The Theory and Application of Multinational Corporate Governance

Runhui Lin · Jean Jinghan Chen

The Theory and Application of Multinational Corporate Governance

palgrave
macmillan

Runhui Lin
Business School
Nankai University
Tianjin, China

Jean Jinghan Chen
University of Macao
Macao, China

ISBN 978-981-16-7702-1   ISBN 978-981-16-7703-8 (eBook)
https://doi.org/10.1007/978-981-16-7703-8

© The Editor(s) (if applicable) and The Author(s), under exclusive license to Springer Nature Singapore Pte Ltd. 2022
This work is subject to copyright. All rights are solely and exclusively licensed by the Publisher, whether the whole or part of the material is concerned, specifically the rights of translation, reprinting, reuse of illustrations, recitation, broadcasting, reproduction on microfilms or in any other physical way, and transmission or information storage and retrieval, electronic adaptation, computer software, or by similar or dissimilar methodology now known or hereafter developed.
The use of general descriptive names, registered names, trademarks, service marks, etc. in this publication does not imply, even in the absence of a specific statement, that such names are exempt from the relevant protective laws and regulations and therefore free for general use.
The publisher, the authors and the editors are safe to assume that the advice and information in this book are believed to be true and accurate at the date of publication. Neither the publisher nor the authors or the editors give a warranty, expressed or implied, with respect to the material contained herein or for any errors or omissions that may have been made. The publisher remains neutral with regard to jurisdictional claims in published maps and institutional affiliations.

This Palgrave Macmillan imprint is published by the registered company Springer Nature Singapore Pte Ltd.
The registered company address is: 152 Beach Road, #21-01/04 Gateway East, Singapore 189721, Singapore

Acknowledgements

The authors would like to extend sincere gratitude to the following scholars for their cooperation and assistance in the research leading to this book: Xie Li, Gui Yuan, Wu Jun, Li Na, Zhou Changbao, Song Jingli, Li Kanghong, Li Ya, Li Fei, Xie Zaiyang, and Hongjuan Zhang. The authors take full responsibility for any errors that remain. We are grateful for the financial support provided by the Natural Science Foundation of China (NSFC: 71772096, 71132001, 71732005). We also thank for the support provided by China Group Companies Association and a number of business people. Professor Jean Jinghan Chen also acknowledges the University of Macau's Grants SRG2019-00146-FBA and CPG2020-00018-FBA to support this book publication.

Contents

1 **Introduction**   1
   References   4

2 **MNEs and Multinational Corporate Governance**   5
  2.1 *MNE Development and Theoretical Research*   6
    2.1.1 *The Emergence and Development of MNEs*   6
    2.1.2 *Theoretical Research into MNEs*   9
  2.2 *Overview of Corporate Governance Studies*   11
    2.2.1 *Corporate Governance—Theoretical Framework and Essential Issues*   11
    2.2.2 *Traditional Corporate Governance Versus Multinational Corporate Governance*   15
  2.3 *Multinational Corporate Governance—Connotations and Research Progress*   16
    2.3.1 *Connotations*   16
    2.3.2 *The Necessity of Multinational Corporate Governance Studies*   17
    2.3.3 *Institutional Factors Affecting Multinational Corporate Governance*   18
    2.3.4 *Main Topics in Multinational Corporate Governance Studies*   19
  References   22

3 Theoretical Framework for Multinational Corporate Governance — 25

3.1 Theories Related to the Studies of Multinational Corporate Governance — 26
   3.1.1 Theories Related to Corporate Governance Studies — 27
   3.1.2 Theories Related to MNE Studies — 30

3.2 Characteristics of Multinational Corporate Governance — 33
   3.2.1 Network Governance Attributes — 34
   3.2.2 Extended Agency Chain — 34
   3.2.3 Expanded Connotations of Internal and External Governance — 35
   3.2.4 Cultural Dominance in Multinational Corporate Governance — 35

3.3 Basic Theories and Framework for Multinational Corporate Governance — 36
   3.3.1 Stakeholder Theory — 36
   3.3.2 Agency Theory — 38
   3.3.3 Institutional Design Theory — 39
   3.3.4 Decision-Making Theory — 40
   3.3.5 Network Governance Theory — 41

References — 43

4 Multinational Corporate Governance: A Network Governance Framework — 45

4.1 MNE Network Node Governance — 47
   4.1.1 Parent Company Governance — 47
   4.1.2 Foreign Subsidiary Governance — 53

4.2 MNEs Network Relationship Governance: Parent-Subsidiary Relationship Governance — 57
   4.2.1 Parent Company Strategy and Parent-Subsidiary Governance — 57
   4.2.2 Parent Company Control and Subsidiary Ownership Governance — 59

4.3 MNEs External Network Governance — 60
   4.3.1 Host Country Institutional and Cultural Influences on Foreign Subsidiary Governance — 64

		4.3.2	Influence of Host Country Stakeholders on MNEs	65
	4.4		Multinational Corporate Governance: An Integrated Network Governance Framework	66
	References			67
5	**Foreign Subsidiary Governance**			75
	5.1		Internal Governance of Foreign Subsidiaries of MNEs	76
		5.1.1	Board Governance	76
		5.1.2	Equity Governance	78
		5.1.3	Senior Management Governance	81
	5.2		Parent-Subsidiary Relationship Governance	82
		5.2.1	Parent-Subsidiary Relationship Governance of MNEs in Developed Countries	82
		5.2.2	Parent-Subsidiary Relationship Governance of MNEs in Emerging Markets	84
	5.3		External Governance of Foreign Subsidiaries	84
		5.3.1	How Host Country Stakeholders Affect Foreign Subsidiaries	85
		5.3.2	How Host Countries' Institutions and Cultures Affect Foreign Subsidiaries	85
	References			87
6	**Institutional Distance, Cultural Distance, and MNEs Governance**			93
	6.1		Factors Influencing MNEs Governance	93
		6.1.1	Influencing Factors of MNEs Governance at the Macro Level	94
		6.1.2	Influencing Factors of MNEs Governance at the Meso-Level	96
		6.1.3	Influencing Factors of MNEs Governance at the Micro-Level	96
	6.2		Institutional Distance and MNEs Governance	97
		6.2.1	Institutional Distance and Host Country Selection	98
		6.2.2	Institutional Distance and Choice of Entry Mode by Foreign Subsidiaries	101
		6.2.3	Institutional Distance and the Legitimacy of Foreign Subsidiaries	104

6.3		Cultural Distance and MNEs Governance	106
	6.3.1	Cultural Distance and the Choice of Host Country	107
	6.3.2	Cultural Distance and the Choice of Foreign Market Entry Mode	108
	6.3.3	Cultural Distance and the Legitimacy of Foreign Subsidiaries	110
References			111

7 The Institutional Gap and Chinese MNEs Governance — 117

7.1	The Institutional Gap		117
	7.1.1	Conceptual Role of the Institutional Gap	117
	7.1.2	Connotations of the Institutional Gap	118
7.2	Institutional Gap and MNEs Governance		120
	7.2.1	Institutional Deficit and MNEs Governance	120
	7.2.2	Institutional Surplus and MNEs Governance	122
	7.2.3	Institutional Similarity and MNEs Governance	123
7.3	The Institutional Gap and the Governance of Equity Ownership in Foreign Subsidiaries of Chinese MNEs		124
	7.3.1	Formal Institution Deficit and the Governance of Equity Ownership in Foreign Subsidiaries of Chinese MNEs	124
	7.3.2	Formal Institutional Surplus and the Governance of Equity Ownership in Foreign Subsidiaries of Chinese MNEs	125
	7.3.3	Informal Institutional Differences and the Governance of Equity Ownership in Foreign Subsidiaries of Chinese MNEs	126
	7.3.4	Host Country Institutions, the Institutional Gap, and the Governance of Equity Ownership in Foreign Subsidiaries of Chinese MNEs	128
	7.3.5	Diversification Strategy, the Institutional Gap, and the Governance of Equity Ownership in Foreign Subsidiaries of Chinese MNEs	130
7.4	The Institutional Gap and Market Performance of Chinese Overseas Listed Companies		132

		7.4.1	Political Connections and Enterprise Value on IPO	132
		7.4.2	Moderating Effect of the Institutional Environment on the Relationship Between Political Connections and Enterprise Value on IPO	134
		7.4.3	Comparing Investors in Foreign and Domestic Markets on Their Sensitivity to the Relationship Between Political Connections and Enterprise Value on IPO	136
	References			137
8	Governance Structure and Mechanism of Chinese MNEs			143
	8.1	Governance Structure of Chinese MNEs		143
		8.1.1	Rights and Interests of Controlling Shareholders and Minority Shareholders	143
		8.1.2	Board of Directors	145
		8.1.3	Managers and Executive Pay	146
		8.1.4	Stakeholders	149
	8.2	Governance Mechanism of Chinese MNEs		150
		8.2.1	Internal Governance Mechanism of Chinese MNEs	151
		8.2.2	External Governance Mechanism of Chinese MNEs	151
	References			155
9	Path and Characteristics of the Multinational Governance of Chinese Enterprises			159
	9.1	Process and Theoretical Development of China's Multinational Corporate Governance		160
		9.1.1	Process of China's Multinational Corporate Governance	160
		9.1.2	Theoretical Development of Multinational Governance	173
	9.2	Evolution of China's Multinational Corporate Governance		175
		9.2.1	Development of Drivers of International Business	175
		9.2.2	Changes in the Host Country Selection	176

	9.2.3	Changes in the Entry Modes	178
	9.2.4	Change of Parent-Subsidiary Governance Mode	181
	9.2.5	Development of Governance Structures	182
	References		186
10	**Conclusions**		**187**
	10.1	Multinational Corporate Governance Theories: Predecessors and Developments	188
	10.2	Network-Based Analytical Framework for Multinational Corporate Governance Studies	189
	10.3	Two Key Issues in Multinational Corporate Governance	190
	10.4	Experience of and Aspirations for China's Multinational Corporate Governance Practices	191
	References		192

List of Figures

Fig. 3.1	Stakeholders of an MNE	37
Fig. 3.2	Agency chain of an MNE	38
Fig. 3.3	Network structures in which the foreign subsidiaries of MNEs are embedded	42
Fig. 4.1	Interaction between MNEs and host country environment	61
Fig. 4.2	MNE network governance framework	67
Fig. 6.1	Framework of factors influencing MNE governance	94
Fig. 9.1	Changes in the number of host countries for investment, 2005–2015	177
Fig. 9.2	Geographical distribution of China's outward investment in 2015	177
Fig. 9.3	Choice of stock exchanges for Chinese IPOs overseas, 2000–2015	180
Fig. 9.4	Ways of listing overseas for Chinese companies, 2005–2015	181
Fig. 9.5	Overseas directors, independent directors, and executives in Chinese listed companies, 2008–2015	184
Fig. 9.6	Proportion and types of directors with overseas backgrounds in Chinese listed companies, 2015	184
Fig. 10.1	MNE networks	190

List of Tables

Table 9.1	The changing role of government in China's multinational corporate governance	163
Table 9.2	Milestones in Chinese MNEs' multinational corporate governance	167
Table 9.3	Changes in the driving forces of Chinese MNEs' multinational operations	176
Table 9.4	Major overseas M&A deals (worth over US$1 billion) by Chinese companies in 2015	180

CHAPTER 1

Introduction

Multinational corporations (MNEs) originated from the seaborne trade in the colonial period before the Industrial Revolution. The Dutch East India Company, founded in 1602, can be considered the world's first MNE. As their operation and management span two or more countries, MNEs are also known as transnational enterprises, international firms, supernational enterprises, and cosmo-corporations.

MNEs are a telling sign of trade globalisation. Recent centuries have witnessed the rise of MNEs successively in Europe and America, Japan and South Korea, and China. European and American MNEs dominated the global market until the 1950s when Japanese companies started to globalise. In the 1970s and 1980s, many South Korean companies also began to grow their global presence. After 2000, MNEs from emerging markets appeared on the global stage, and there was exceptionally robust growth in companies from emerging markets, represented by China, after the 2008 global financial crisis. These companies continued to expand their global reach and scale up their operations, and 124 companies based in mainland China and Hong Kong recorded the enviable achievement of being listed in the 2020 Fortune Global 500, exceeding the 121 companies from the US. The rise of Chinese MNEs has become a major driving force of global economic growth and technological advances.

© The Author(s), under exclusive license to Springer Nature Singapore Pte Ltd. 2022
R. Lin and J. J. Chen, *The Theory and Application of Multinational Corporate Governance*, https://doi.org/10.1007/978-981-16-7703-8_1

As globalisation has accelerated, MNEs, born during the early evolution of the modern economy, have become the main engine of the global economy, technical advancement, and product innovation, playing a pivotal role in the world economy and the global technological revolution. However, MNEs are also often embroiled in financial fraud and corporate scandals. The Enron financial fraud scandal and the BP oil spill left the world in deep shock. Such scandals not only taint the reputation of the home country but also cause economic or environmental loss to the host country and ultimately impede globalisation. Therefore, MNEs should improve corporate governance and organisational innovation from the inside as regulatory systems are enhanced from the outside. As increasing numbers of MNEs from emerging markets, such as China, India, and Brazil, step into the spotlight, the new industrial revolution led by informatisation closes the gap between developed and emerging countries, thus intensifying their competition. Meanwhile, as COVID-19 runs rampant globally, populism and deglobalisation have resurged, and protectionism and unilateralism exert negative impacts on the world economy. The world is facing a period of major change unlike anything seen since World War II. Achieving sustainable development in this context is a test of a company's management and governance abilities.

We argue that corporate governance is a major challenge that many MNEs face due to the sophistication of MNEs and the complexity and significance of this issue in an overseas context. Compared to typical domestic companies, MNEs feature a greater diversity of cultures, shareholders, and employees. Institutions are nested and isomorphic with each other at multiple levels. Diverse institutions and cultures, a broader range of stakeholders, and more severe information asymmetry make governing MNEs more complex than general companies. Sound multinational governance is therefore of great importance for MNEs. Multinational corporate governance has been extensively studied from the perspectives of institutional theory (DiMaggio & Powell, 1983; Scott, 1995), stakeholder theory (Freeman, 2010), upper echelons theory (Hambrick & Mason, 1984), and signal theory (Spence, 1973). These studies have laid a good foundation regarding the object, level, and content of study; however, they are fragmented and lack a systematic outlook. To benefit MNE governance, we call for theoretical innovation to break free of the limitations of business globalisation theories and enhance governance analysis and studies, which is also this book's purpose.

This book is divided into nine chapters. This chapter introduces the development and governance framework of MNEs and presents the book's structure. Chapter 2 reviews the generation and development of MNEs, outlines the system of concepts and theoretical framework for multinational corporate governance studies, and lists the field's connotations, research progress, and main research questions. Chapter 3 presents the theoretical framework for multinational corporate governance. We review the principal-agent theory, stewardship theory, stakeholder theory, and corporate system theory in relation to the multinational corporate governance and arrive at the characteristics of the multinational corporate governance and the theoretical basis and research framework for studying the topic. Chapter 4 introduces the network governance framework for MNEs. In summarising the literature on multinational corporate governance, we find that most studies ignore that an MNE exists as a network organisation. From the perspective of network governance, this chapter elaborates on the governance of network nodes (parent company and foreign subsidiaries), governance of network relationship (parent-subsidiary and subsidiary-subsidiary relationship), and governance of external factors (host and home country institutions, international organisations, and other external stakeholders), thus forming a comprehensive MNE network governance framework. Chapter 5 covers the governance of foreign subsidiaries of MNEs. This chapter reviews and comments on the internal and external governance of foreign subsidiaries and the governance of the relationship between foreign subsidiaries and the parent company. Chapter 6 investigates the relevance of institutional and cultural distance to MNE governance. This chapter first establishes a three-level (macro-meso-micro) framework to describe factors affecting MNE governance, discusses the relationship between institutional and cultural distance and multinational corporate governance, and further discusses the relationship between institutional and cultural distance and the governance of Chinese MNEs. Chapter 7 addresses institutional gaps and Chinese MNEs. This chapter first discusses the influence of institutional deficit and institutional surplus on the selection of outward foreign direct investment (OFDI) location, host country, and equity entry mode in multinational corporate governance. It then analyses the relationships between the gaps in formal and informal institutions, the overseas equity governance of Chinese MNEs, and the performance of Chinese overseas listed companies. Chapter 8 covers the governance structure and mechanism of Chinese MNEs. This chapter first discusses and analyses the governance structure of Chinese MNEs, including shareholder governance, board governance, TMT governance, and stakeholder governance, and then discusses and analyses internal and external aspects of the governance mechanism of Chinese MNEs. Chapter 9 identifies the approach to and characteristics of the multinational governance of Chinese MNEs. This chapter tracks the history of and research developments in Chinese corporate multinational governance and analyses five aspects of the evolution of the Chinese corporate multinational governance approach: multinational motivation, host country selection, entry mode selection, parent-subsidiary governance model, and governance structure. The end of the chapter summarises the theoretical framework for MNE governance proposed in this book.

References

DiMaggio, P. J., & Powell, W. W. (1983). The iron cage revisited: Institutional isomorphism and collective rationality in organizational fields. *American Sociological Review, 48*(2), 147–160.

Freeman, R. E. (2010). *Strategic management: A stakeholder approach.* Cambridge University Press.

Hambrick, D. C., & Mason, P. A. (1984). Upper echelons: The organization as a reflection of its top managers. *Academy of Management Review, 2*(9), 193–207.

Scott, W. R. (1995). *Institutions and organization: Ideas, interests and identities.* Sage.

Spence, M. (1973). Job market signaling. *Quarterly Journal of Economics, 87*(3), 355–374.

CHAPTER 2

MNEs and Multinational Corporate Governance

In the wake of the major geographical discoveries of the fifteenth century, the world became more connected. Cultural and trade exchanges multiplied, colonialism and trade liberalism appeared in succession, and a unified global market finally took shape. All countries and regions became part of an international system for the division of labour.

Today, as economic globalisation deepens, economies around the world are becoming more mutually dependent. MNEs have accelerated economic globalisation, which has allowed the MNEs to expand their global reach and improve their competitive edge by creating favourable conditions for the release of market forces. MNEs have undergone different stages of development during the process of economic globalisation. MNE governance theory, the study of applying corporate governance theory to MNEs, has also taken shape. Its theoretical bases are mainly MNE and corporate governance theories. This chapter tracks the history of MNEs against the backdrop of economic globalisation, elaborates on MNE theory developments, and proposes new priorities for MNE research.

2.1 MNE Development and Theoretical Research

2.1.1 The Emergence and Development of MNEs

Globalisation is one of the most important features and trends of the world economy today. Economic globalisation, which accelerated in the 1990s, is primarily an economic process of interaction and integration, and it involves how countries and people correlate with, influence, and restrict each other in politics, culture, technology, military endeavours, security, ideology, lifestyle, and values. There are ten general aspects of globalisation: technology, economics, politics, law, management, organisations, culture, ideology, interpersonal communications, and international relations. Economic globalisation facilitates the allocation of resources and production factors across the globe, the flow of capital and products, the spread of technology, and the economic development of less-developed regions. It represents progress in human development and is an irresistible trend of the global economy.

As technology advances and countries become more interdependent, MNEs play an increasingly important role in the global economy. Economic globalisation presents an excellent opportunity for MNEs, driving economic growth as vital entities in international trade, finance, economic, and technical cooperation and competition. As a new corporate form emerging against the background of globalisation, MNEs coordinate resources across the globe to create maximum value. It is fair to say that they are an inevitable result of globalisation.

Any change in their development, especially strategic adjustments and restructuring, dramatically influences the international market or the global economy. Since the 1990s, MNEs have been shifting from capital-intensive businesses to knowledge- and technology-intensive businesses, from manufacturing to services, and from hardware to software, which has induced the adjustment and cross-border transfer of industries worldwide. While giving full play to the core business, they also intervene in upstream and downstream businesses to secure control over core technologies. MNEs transfer or localise downstream technologies to restructure their business. By setting up foreign subsidiaries, they are able to bypass many barriers and rapidly identify local market needs. They can make full use of local resources and reduce production and trade costs through internal transactions, facilitating production, circulation, and consumption on a global scale and thus bringing about economic globalisation of practical significance. Therefore, MNEs are the carriers and driving force of economic globalisation.

Globalisation started in the fifteenth century when advanced capitalist countries in Europe sought to expand sea trade routes. Emerging in the age of discovery, MNEs have come a long way since the advent of the East India Company in 1600. Generally, their history can be divided into three stages: chartered companies, modern MNEs, and new-era MNEs.

2.1.1.1 Chartered Companies
A chartered company is a type of corporation that emerged during the mercantilist period in the seventeenth and eighteenth centuries. It enjoyed a trading monopoly granted by the sovereign authority of a state in an overseas colony of the state. After discovering the 'New World' of the Americas, Western European countries started colonial trade, and chartered companies replaced individual traders. A chartered company was often incorporated under a royal charter that granted it an exclusive monopoly in a trade destination. Such companies also assumed certain administrative functions and could even make war. For example, the East India Company was founded by Queen Elizabeth I of England to compete with the Netherlands for superiority in international trade. The company started the Battle of Plassey in India in 1757 and gradually encroached into India's territory. By 1820, India had been entirely colonised by Great Britain. Several other chartered companies were also famous at this time, including the Royal African Company, Hudson's Bay Company, and the Dutch East India Company. Chartered companies primarily engaged in trading and shipping, and although they gradually expanded into finance, most focused on transporting raw materials, which suggests that they were trade organisations in essence. Manufacturing was generally limited to small workshops in Western Europe, and the absence of the factory system and mass production made it impossible to build a multinational manufacturing chain. The theory of comparative advantage developed by David Ricardo explains why chartered companies emerged. According to this theory, even when a country has an absolute disadvantage in all goods, it still can benefit from exporting to another country as long as it has a relative cost advantage.

2.1.1.2 Modern MNEs

In 1856, the UK promulgated the *Joint Stock Companies Act*. The emergence of joint-stock companies marked the birth of modern companies and the beginning of a gradual improvement in the corporate governance structure. The ability of joint-stock companies to mobilise and pool funds from all sectors of society laid a solid foundation for them to grow into MNEs. During the Second Industrial Revolution, which started around 1870, large factories gradually established a manufacturing system, the international division of labour deepened, and railway, telegraph, and ship technologies advanced. The combination of these factors made multinational operations possible. American and European companies began to set up foreign facilities or subsidiaries, expanding their market and production to foreign countries. Raw materials were transported from all over the world to their global factories, where products were manufactured or processed and sold worldwide. A global industrial chain took shape. Modern MNEs featuring multinational manufacturing took the place of chartered companies and became major players in the global economic arena. A new technological revolution picked up steam after the Second World War, and a host of technologies represented by computer information technology have continuously reshaped the global industrial landscape since then. The development of the Internet, container transportation, and international aviation has created the conditions for an international division of labour. In addition, the ambition of developed countries to reach global markets and the free trade policies adopted by developing countries has further boosted the development of MNEs, which have become the driving force and an integral part of the global economy. However, multinational operations pose a new challenge to corporate governance.

2.1.1.3 New-Era MNEs

Since the beginning of the twenty-first century, information technology has changed the world in unprecedented ways, and MNEs are also taking on new features. First, they are gradually weakening their identity with their home country to seek an optimal allocation of resources worldwide. They are working to build a global value chain and enhance 'borderless' openness to maximise the benefits of globalisation. According to *World Investment Report 2020*, International production by MNEs accounts for a significant share of the global economy. Some 80 per cent of the global trade is linked to the international production networks of MNEs. The combined value-added generated by MNEs in their home countries and foreign affiliates amounts to about a quarter of the global GDP and about a third of the private-sector output. MNEs' investment decisions largely shape the trade-in value-added (TiVA) model in global value chains. MNEs coordinate global value chains through a complex supplier network and various governance models, including direct ownership of foreign subsidiaries, contractual relationships, and routine transactions. These governance models and the resulting power structure significantly impact the distribution of economic benefits from trade in the global value chain and their long-term development implications. However, several financial crises since 1997 have caused people to reflect more critically on globalisation. Increasing numbers of people in developing countries express their discontent with MNEs' manufacturing plants, and compliance issues are becoming increasingly prominent.

2.1.2 Theoretical Research into MNEs

MNEs are attracting increasing attention because of their important role in the global economy. As informatisation and globalisation accelerate, MNEs face a more dynamic and complex business environment. Multinational operations, which were once unusual economic phenomena, have become ubiquitous. The rise of MNEs has therefore aroused great interest among researchers. MNE theories primarily address the following three questions: (1) Why do companies invest and operate abroad? (2) In which countries and regions do they invest and operate? (3) How should they invest and operate to develop a sustainable competitive advantage?

The mainstream MNE theories were developed during the massive growth and expansion of large Western MNEs in the 1960s. Therefore, they mainly analyse and explain how large companies with monopoly power went overseas for the first time and developed a global presence, traditional advantages. The global promotion model is no longer as competitive as before, and MNEs need to develop new competitive edges. MNE theories are therefore closely related to the times in which they are formulated and need to evolve with the changing reality.

According to the monopolistic advantage theory, developed by Hymer (1960), an MNE with monopoly power in its home country tends to extend its monopolistic advantages or privileges to foreign countries (i.e., host countries), where it works to achieve the monopoly position and profits that it enjoys in its home country in a bid to create an oligopoly and a collusive network in the global market. The internalisation theory, developed by Buckley and Casson (1976), claimed that the essence of MNEs is the result of the internationalisation of the cross-border market. MNEs eliminate efficiency distortions caused by imperfect market competition by internalising intermediate product markets. The boundaries of an MNE are determined by the marginal cost of external transactions and the cost of internal coordination. The eclectic paradigm of international production put forward by Dunning (1988) held that for companies to invest abroad, they must have ownership, location, and internalisation advantages.

The four 'Asian Tigers' (Hong Kong, Singapore, South Korea, and Taiwan) emerged as significant sources of foreign direct investments (FDI) after the 1980s. This phenomenon drew the attention of economists, who then carried out research and developed a range of theories, including the small-scale technology theory (Wells, 1977), technology localisation theory (Lall, 1983), and the theory of technological innovation and industrial upgrading (Cantwell, 1994; Tolentino, 1993). Breaking the assumptions of monopoly advantage and market imperfection held by classic theories, these theories proposed that small-scale technology, technology localisation, and dynamic industrial upgrades lay the foundation for FDI. The FDI path theory (Dunning, 1998) and the competitive advantage theory (Porter, 1990) correlate the FDI process with the national economy, industrial development stages, and industrial competitiveness. These factors can explain FDI activity at different stages in different countries to some extent. Studies in this period were no longer limited to static description; they explored the significance of investment experience and technical accumulations in the business activities of companies in developing countries, described the phases of FDI of a country based on macroeconomic variables, and made investment forecasts.

Overall, studies of MNE theories can be divided into three categories. The first one is based on the industrial organisation theory and imperfect competition. The main theories developed in this category include monopolistic advantage theory and internalisation theory. The second category is based on international trade theory and perfect competition. Representative theories include product life cycle theory and comparative advantage theory. The third category is based on corporate management, organisation, and strategy theories. The first two categories are traditional or mainstream MNE theories, whereas the latest theories, such as organisational learning theory and real options theory, fit into the third category. We can see that researchers have gradually shifted their focus to studying how MNEs can sustain their competitive advantages based on theories of corporate management, organisations, and strategy. As an important branch of business management, corporate governance involves a set of systems designed to facilitate wise decision-making and coordinate the relationship between stakeholders. How MNEs can design a reasonable governance framework based on corporate governance theories to ensure a sustainable competitive advantage is an important research topic.

2.2 Overview of Corporate Governance Studies

2.2.1 *Corporate Governance—Theoretical Framework and Essential Issues*

2.2.1.1 *System of Concepts*

In the 1930s, US scholars Berle and Means (1932) first declared the separation of ownership and control in modern companies, which drew people's attention to agency problems. Williamson (1975) developed the theory of the firm as a governance structure. Fama and Jensen (1983) carried out a detailed study of agency conflicts and costs and proposed the theoretical basis and research framework for corporate governance. Later, Western scholars conducted extensive research on the connotations of corporate governance. Shleifer and Vishny (1997) conducted a theoretical review and argued that corporate governance is a means of ensuring that capital providers can get a return on their investments in a company. Apart from theoretical studies, scholars have also explored operational issues. For example, Zahra and Pearce (1989) studied board structures and mechanisms, Gillan and Starks (2007) studied the role of shareholders and institutional investors, and Harris and Helfat (1998) studied the governance of managers.

According to Oliver Hart (1995), two problems inevitably cause corporate governance problems in an organisation: (1) agency problems, conflicts of interests between members of an organisation, and (2) transaction cost problems, when transaction costs are so high that agency problems cannot be settled by contract. Cochran and Wartick

(1988)[1] proposed that corporate governance involves specific problems arising from the interaction between executives, shareholders, directors, and other stakeholders. Corporate governance problems arise when the actual beneficiaries of a decision/action are not the expected beneficiaries. Qian (1995) proposed that a corporate governance structure includes a set of systems designed to manage the relationship between interested groups in a company, including investors, managers, and employees and help each group realise its economic benefits. A corporate governance structure should specify how to allocate and exercise control rights, supervise and evaluate the board of directors, managers, and employees, and design and implement incentive mechanisms. In the narrow sense, corporate governance is a mechanism for a company's owners, primarily the shareholders, to supervise its operators. It should reasonably allocate rights and obligations between the owners and the operators through a set of systems and aim to ensure the maximum realisation of the shareholders' interests and prevent operators from acting against the owners' interests. It features an internal governance structure consisting of the board of shareholders, board of directors, board of supervisors, and management. General corporate governance involves a broader range of stakeholders, including shareholders, creditors, suppliers, employees, governments, communities, and other interested groups. In summary, corporate governance is a set of formal and informal systems used to coordinate the relationship between a company and all interested parties to ensure wise decision-making and protect the company's interests.

2.2.1.2 Theoretical Framework

Due to the division of labour and specialisation, modern corporations are subject to a separation between ownership and control, which gives rise to agency costs despite increasing operational efficiency. The purpose of corporate governance studies is to decrease these agency costs by designing effective supervision and incentive mechanisms without compromising the increased efficiency associated with the division of labour and specialisation. Therefore, corporate governance has become a major focus of modern corporate studies.

From the Chinese perspective, foreign studies of corporate governance have mainly focused on how to supervise and control the behaviour of

---

[1] Cochran P. L., Wartick S. L. Corporate governance: A review of the literature. Financial Executives Research Foundation, 1988.

managers and how to protect the interests of stakeholders. Domestic studies are centred on how to tackle severe corruption among managers in state-owned enterprises (SOEs) during the SOE reform and how to establish a modern corporate system for SOEs, as well as how to control the ethical risks for shareholders of listed companies and how to govern family companies and private companies.

A corporate governance system covers internal and external governance. Internal governance involves a set of formal systems defined by the *Company Law* and constituting the basis of corporate governance. It helps achieve equilibrium between the board of shareholders, board of directors, board of supervisors, and management. In contrast, external governance focuses on adapting companies to market competition through a reversed transmission of market pressure. Shareholders/potential shareholders and creditors connect to a company primarily through the capital market, whereas operators, employees, and customers connect primarily through the labour and product markets. Market competition necessitates an incentive mechanism that spurs companies to choose sound corporate governance systems. The government, which partly replaces the market, is also an essential external variable in corporate governance.

In summary, internal governance primarily focuses on board size, ownership structure, and managerial incentives, whereas external governance involves government regulation and laws.

(1) Internal Governance

The ownership structure is the most important of the internal factors affecting corporate governance mechanisms. Starting from the separation of ownership and control discovered by Berle and Means (1932), traditional corporate governance studies were focused on analysing and optimising internal governance mechanisms, such as the board of directors and management. More recent studies cover issues related to the conflict between majority shareholders and minority shareholders, personal benefits of controlling shareholders, and inheritance of special assets in family companies arising while creating governance models in the context of ownership concentration from a systematic perspective.

As a vital internal governance mechanism, the board of directors has the two major functions of guidance and supervision. Researchers have studied how the board of directors functions and how to improve its efficiency from various perspectives. Over the past decade, the board of directors has been a particular source of academic interest, and the research focus has shifted from its basic features to its social networks and interactions with management.

Studies of the governance of senior management cover managerial incentives and restraint mechanisms, issues related to their social networks, and their interactions with other managerial teams. Generally, top management pay remains a subject of concern.

(2) External Governance

Traditional external variables have been gradually introduced into corporate governance studies to analyse the influence of the institutional environment on corporate governance models. These variables reflect aspects of various domains, including law, political relations, stakeholders, institutional investors, and media.

A group of researchers including La Porta, Lopez-de-Silanes, Shleifer, and Vishny included law as a factor in corporate governance studies. They proposed that laws in different countries have different requirements and provide different degrees of protection for investors. Companies in different countries, therefore, have different ownership structures and hence different governance models. Given that such differences affect the performance of corporate governance mechanisms, the law should be considered an important factor in corporate governance studies.

Political connections produce informal institutional incentives and governance effects and function as an informal governance mechanism. Studies centred on this mechanism explore how majority shareholders, the board of directors, or management obtain benefits such as preferential financing by establishing political connections against a specific institutional background. Political connections bring benefits and risks to corporate governance, and their influence on corporate performance is complicated.

Increasing attention is now being paid to stakeholder theory, which further expands the boundaries of corporate governance studies by considering creditors, employees, suppliers, communities, and the business environment as falling under the protection of companies. The stakeholder governance mechanism induces or forces management to internalise the benefits of these stakeholders. The theory holds that stakeholders' rights and interests need to be supported by controlling managerial behaviour in corporate governance.

Studies of capital markets focus on the role of institutional investors. Their supervision is one of the governance mechanisms used to ease agency conflicts. Institutional investors are not only able to participate in the decision-making of a company that they have a stake in but also to influence managers' decisions by trading stocks. Researchers are more interested in the role of institutional investors in dealing with the first category of agency problems than the second category.

Global studies of external corporate governance also consider media governance. Through their agenda-setting capabilities, media outlets can affect a company's reputation and its managers and directors and thus play a role in corporate governance.

2.2.2 Traditional Corporate Governance Versus Multinational Corporate Governance

The expanding organisational boundaries of MNEs have given rise to a series of corporate governance problems. A propensity for integration blurs the boundaries between parent companies and subsidiaries. As a result, international legal systems face many conflicts when determining the responsibilities of MNEs and, for the sake of corporate reputation, parent companies usually take responsibility for subsidiary activities. With an extended group of stakeholders, MNEs should make a prudent choice of organisational structure and continuously innovate their corporate governance mechanisms to better handle their relationship with partners, allies, suppliers, and employees in host countries. Multinational corporate governance expands and enriches corporate governance theories in three ways. First, it involves entities at the national level (the home and host countries) and the corporate level (parent companies and their foreign subsidiaries). Second, it expands the boundaries of corporate governance to include foreign countries, which stretches the agency chain and increases the difficulty and cost of governance. Third, it expands the group of stakeholders to include those in both the home and host countries, complicating external systems and the business environment.

As an interfirm organisation, a business group can either comprise a parent company and one or more subsidiaries or a group of horizontally affiliated companies. As member companies are legally independent and characterised by information asymmetry, parent companies and subsidiaries suffer from agency problems arising from their equity relationship. Furthermore, affiliated companies face trust and cooperation problems due to their possession of unique resources that are hard to copy. Sound group governance mechanisms are needed to solve these problems. There are also agency problems between majority shareholders, such as parent companies and minority shareholders. Parent companies may harm the interests of other stakeholders out of self-interest, which adds to the complexity of group governance. Overall, group governance involves the top-down governance of subsidiaries by parent companies, the initiatives of subsidiaries, and the two-way governance between parent companies and subsidiaries.

As understanding of the interaction between environmental factors and internal motives has deepened, network organisations have attracted increasing attention from the academic community. Jones et al. (1997) summarised nine descriptions of network governance in *A General Theory of Network Governance*. He held that network governance involves a select, persistent, and structured set of independent enterprises (and non-profit agencies) engaged in creating products or services based on implicit and open-ended contracts to adapt to environmental contingencies and to coordinate and safeguard exchanges, with these contracts being socially, not legally, binding. In a study on the future development of corporate governance, Li et al. (2003) identified two approaches to network governance: governing by network and governing network organisations. Most researchers have focused on the latter, leaving limited literature on the former. The purpose of network governance studies is to define the different forms of networks and to illustrate the value of networks as a tool of governance applicable to different types of entities at different levels for achieving network goals.

2.3 Multinational Corporate Governance—Connotations and Research Progress

2.3.1 Connotations

Multinational corporate governance is the governance structure of MNEs and is complicated by their cross-border nature. Multinational corporate governance deals with the governance of parent companies and the relationship between parent companies and subsidiaries and is set in a cross-border context involving a range of issues related to stakeholders. It is essentially a compound mode of corporate governance of an expanded group of entities, at home and abroad and at multiple levels.

Multinational corporate governance involves parent companies, subsidiaries, the relationship between parent companies and subsidiaries, and multinational group networks. There are two principal-agent relationships involved in MNEs. First, shareholders are the original principals, and the management is the agents, as is the case in general companies. Second, parent companies are the direct principals, and foreign subsidiaries are the agents. Parent companies and subsidiaries form a cascading agency chain and face prominent agency problems due to information asymmetry resulting from the long distance between them and institutional and cultural differences between home and host countries.

As MNEs develop, their groups of potential stakeholders expand to include those beyond their normal area of business. The interests of many stakeholders are significantly affected by an MNE's employment, technology transfer, trade creation, and tax effects. MNEs have a remarkable and profound influence on economic development in developing countries in particular. Multinational governance primarily deals with the dynamic interactions among various stakeholders, including home countries, host countries, parent companies, subsidiaries, and partner companies. Unlike the single corporation's governance, multinational corporate governance is network governance in essence.

2.3.2 *The Necessity of Multinational Corporate Governance Studies*

Economic globalisation presents challenges for corporate governance both within countries and across borders. The former is an essential precondition for MNEs' global operations, and the latter determines whether MNEs can successfully invest and operate across the globe. Multinational corporate governance studies are necessary for the following two major reasons.

First, companies should cater to the need for global governance created by economic globalisation. Multinational capital has become a necessary spur for economic growth, and economic globalisation demands changes in global economic governance. The contest for factors of production with liquidity is increasingly fierce. In combination, these factors drive the reform of corporate governance models. Economic globalisation influences the governance model of a company by affecting its equity financing, ownership structure, and overseas mergers and acquisitions

(M&A). To adapt to globalisation trends, companies must change their governance models to become competitive globally, which necessitates studies of issues related to multinational corporate governance.

Second, MNEs themselves need such studies. MNEs play an important role in the global economy, and how well corporate governance is executed determines whether they can accomplish their globalising strategies. With a long history, MNEs have developed sophisticated corporate governance structures and accumulated extensive experience in governing foreign subsidiaries. However, they also encounter many problems with corporate governance that enhanced studies on multinational corporate governance structures can help solve.

2.3.3 Institutional Factors Affecting Multinational Corporate Governance

According to neo-institutional theory, institutions are mainly country-specific, regulative, cognitive, and normative. They reflect the rules of the game that companies must follow when doing business in a given market. An organisation's governance practices are intended to achieve legitimacy (conformity to the rules, norms, and routines in the organisational institutional environment) through adaptation to the local institutional environment. MNEs confront many different and possibly conflicting institutions because of the interrelations between home countries, host countries, parent companies, subsidiaries, and partners. Each foreign subsidiary is confronted with two distinct sets of isomorphic pressures and a need to maintain legitimacy within both the host country and the MNE, and such institutional duality affects cross-border governance.

The home and host countries have different institutional environments. Furthermore, institutional environments vary across parent companies, partners in host countries, and subsidiaries. These differences are mainly reflections of institutional and cultural distance. The institutional and cultural distance between the home and host countries intensifies environmental uncertainty and information asymmetry, which adds to the complexity of multinational governance in two ways. First, the agency chain is longer because of expanded national borders, which increases the difficulty and cost of governance; second, a greater diversity of entities is involved in governance, including home and host countries, parent companies, and foreign subsidiaries. MNEs face governance and non-compliance risks both within and outside of their home countries.

Chinese MNEs are presently confronted with various pressures and uncertainties, including maladjustment to different institutions and cultures, market volatility, deglobalisation, China-US trade frictions, new policies on the Belt and Road Initiative, and existing and potential rivals. All of these factors influence aspects of multinational corporate governance, such as creating a proper equity governance model and designing a reasonable system of the board of directors for subsidiaries.

2.3.4 Main Topics in Multinational Corporate Governance Studies

2.3.4.1 Impact of Host Country Institutional Environment on the Governance of Foreign Subsidiaries

Without considering the influence of the institutional environment, MNE governance is just like group governance. MNEs face various institutional environments as they conduct investment, production, operations, and management activities across national borders. In reality, most governance problems confronted by MNEs are associated with the restrictions imposed by institutional environments. A host country only cares about whether the subsidiaries of an MNE conform to applicable regulations in the country and usually pays no attention to the relationship and agreements between these subsidiaries and their parent company. Foreign subsidiaries have to deal with the conflict between their internal governance mechanisms and the host country institutional environment.

2.3.4.2 Evolution of the Role of Subsidiaries and Their Governance Models

The role of foreign subsidiaries changes with the parent company's strategic motivations and the subsidiary's strength. Usually, the governance of foreign subsidiaries evolves from being dominated by the parent company (full compliance) through incomplete governance (relatively independent) to complete governance (central leadership). The governance of foreign subsidiaries in their fledgling stage is dominated by the parent company. Subsidiaries in this stage have only a simple governance structure and incomplete governance mechanisms and are therefore primarily subject to the external governance controls of the parent company. In this governance model, boards of directors are usually small but nimble, incentive, and financial audit mechanisms are easily put into place, and subsidiaries can easily align with the parent company. However, this model cannot meet the development needs of subsidiaries. Foreign subsidiaries are usually held back by this model and may experience a loss of control without the parent company's governance. Therefore, the governance model of foreign subsidiaries must match their business development.

(1) Ownership structure of foreign subsidiaries

Cross-border investment and ownership restructuring in multinational operations lead to various ownership structures of foreign subsidiaries. When selecting an ownership structure for a foreign subsidiary, an MNE needs to consider multiple factors, such as the ownership structure preferences formed over time, the trading costs, its bargaining power over host countries, the institutional environment in host countries, and the subsidiary's stage of growth. Different ownership structures result in different degrees of control being exercised by the MNE, leading to varying corporate performance depending on the environment that an MNE faces.

(2) Flat organisational structure and the cross-border principal-agent problem

With the emergence of the Internet, a flat organisational structure has proved to be conducive to innovation. However, as the business scale and group of uncontrollable stakeholders expand, MNEs may fall short in the supervision of subsidiaries. A parent company finds it difficult to track the opportunistic behaviours of agents of foreign subsidiaries, which further complicates supervision. Against the background of economic globalisation, parent companies have experienced a weakening of control over their foreign subsidiaries, primarily in equity, human resources, and finance. Therefore, solving the principal-agent problem while maintaining a flat organisational structure has become a new issue in multinational corporate governance.

2.3.4.3 Interstate Relations and Multinational Corporate Governance

Institutional links between countries can be both traditional, such as sharing similar religious beliefs, common languages, and colonial histories, and arranged on the initiative of the two countries, with political relations as an essential bilateral institutional link. A country establishes close or distant political relationships with other countries in formal or informal ways to safeguard national security, promote economic exchange, and expand global influence. Formal relations include forming an alliance and signing a treaty or an agreement, whereas informal relations include the friendship or trust between leaders, which features path dependency. A positive bilateral political relationship can strengthen the understanding, trust, and friendship between two countries and mitigate the threat to a corporate investment of political conflict and bias. It can also win special investment opportunities and property protection for companies in the home country. However, political relationships can change due to power transfers, government changes, territorial disputes, and extreme events. How to coordinate the political relationships between countries is a matter of importance for multinational corporate governance.

2.3.4.4 Institutional Distance and Multinational Corporate Governance

Unlike general companies, MNEs face institutional distance caused by the expansion of institutional boundaries, reflecting the extent of dissimilarity between the regulatory, cognitive, and normative institutions of two countries, such as different national political systems, economic development levels, social and cultural institutions, legal systems, and regulatory environments. Institutional distance between the home and host countries intensifies environmental uncertainty and information asymmetry, adding a degree of complexity to multinational governance. With MNEs facing governance and non-compliance risks outside their own countries, further discussions are needed on how to effectively coordinate internal and external governance mechanisms to improve MNEs' adaptability to institutional and cultural distance.

References

Berle, A., & Means, G. (1932). *The modern corporation and private property*. Commerce Clearing House.

Buckley, P. J., & Casson, M. (1976). *The future of the multinational enterprise*. Holmes and Meier.

Cantwell, J. (1994). Foreign direct investment in developing countries: The case of Latin America. *The Methodological Problems Raised by the Collection of FDI Data//En IRELA*, 9–27.

Cochran, P. L., & Wartick, S. L. (1988). *Corporate governance: A review of the literature*. Financial Executives Research Foundation.

Dunning, J. H. (1988). The eclectic paradigm of international production: A restatement and some possible extensions. *Journal of International Business Studies, 19*(1), 1–31.

Dunning, J. H. (1998). Location and multinational enterprise: A neglected factor. *Journal of International Business Studies, 29*(1), 45–66.

Fama, E. F., & Jensen, M. C. (1983). Separation of ownership and control. *Journal of Law and Economics, 26*(2), 301–325.

Gillan, S. L., & Starks, L. T. (2007). The evolution of shareholder activism in the United States. *Journal of Applied Corporate Finance, 19*(1), 55–73.

Harris, D., & Helfat, C. E. (1998). CEO duality, succession, capabilities and agency theory: Commentary and research agenda. *Strategic Management Journal, 19*(9), 901–904.

Hart, O. (1995). *Firms, contracts, and financial structure*. Oxford University Press.

Hymer, S. H. (1960). *The international operation of national firms: A study of direct foreign investment*. Doctoral dissertation, Massachusetts Institute of Technology.

Hymer, S. H. (1976). *The international operations of national firms: A study of direct foreign investment*. MIT Press.

Jones, C., Hesterly, W., & Borgatti, S. (1997). A general theory of network governance: Exchange conditions and social mechanisms. *The Academy of Management Review, 22*, 911–945.

Lall, S. (1983). *The new multinationals: The spread of third world enterprises[M]*. Chichester.

Li et al. (2003). *Network organization: A new trends in organizational development*. Economic Science Press.

Peng, M. W. (2003). Institutional transitions and strategic choices. *Academy of Management Review, 28*(2), 275–296.

Porter, M. E. (1990). *The competitive advantage of nations*. Free Press, Macmillan.

Qian, Y. (1995). Corporate governance structure reform and financing structure reform. *Economic Research Journal, 1995*(1), 20–29.

Shleifer, A., & Vishny, R. W. (1997). A survey of corporate governance. *The Journal of Finance, 52*(2), 737–783.

Tolentino, P. E. (1993). *Technological innovation and third world multinationals* (pp. 101–104). Routledge Press.

Wells, L. T. (1977). *The internationalization of firms from developing countries.* MIT Press.

Williamson, E. (1975). *Markets and hierarchies: Analysis and antitrust implications, a study in the economics of internal organisation.* Free Press.

Zahra, S. A., & Pearce, J. A. (1989). Boards of directors and corporate financial performance: A review and integrative model. *Journal of Management, 15*(2), 291–334.

CHAPTER 3

Theoretical Framework for Multinational Corporate Governance

Multinational corporate governance expands the boundaries of corporate governance. Relevant theoretical research is still in its early stages, and an appropriate theoretical framework is yet to be established. As the globalisation of Chinese companies deepens, there is a need to establish a scientific theoretical model to help MNEs tackle multinational governance issues and expand the corporate governance theories. Therefore, in this chapter, we introduce the theories related to multinational corporate governance studies before discussing the basic theoretical framework for multinational corporate governance. We also review the development and evolution of MNE studies and extract five research orientations from the literature, covering the relationship between institutional distance and multinational corporate governance, governance of parent companies and subsidiaries, governance of parent-subsidiary relationships, and network governance of multinational business groups. We conclude by presenting a theoretical framework for multinational corporate governance consisting of stakeholder theory, institutional design theory, decision-making theory, network theory, and governance culture theory.

© The Author(s), under exclusive license to Springer Nature Singapore Pte Ltd. 2022
R. Lin and J. J. Chen, *The Theory and Application of Multinational Corporate Governance*, https://doi.org/10.1007/978-981-16-7703-8_3

3.1 Theories Related to the Studies of Multinational Corporate Governance

Corporate governance theories are the theoretical basis for establishing a corporate governance structure and solving corporate governance problems. Corporate governance is a system of institutions, procedures, conventions, policies, laws, and mechanisms—formal or informal, internal or external—by which a company coordinates the relationship between a company and all interested parties (including shareholders, creditors, employees, and potential investors) to ensure wise and effective decision-making and to protect the interests of all parties. In essence, corporate governance is a mechanism for a company's owners (primarily the shareholders) to supervise its operators. It involves reasonably defining and allocating the rights and obligations of the owners and the operators through a set of institutional arrangements to ensure the realisation of the maximum interests of shareholders and prevent operators from acting against the owners' interests. An effective corporate governance mechanism is essential for ensuring smooth corporate globalisation and preventing multinational operation risks. The increasing numbers of companies going global or going public abroad face challenges and risks arising from a series of problems associated with globalisation, such as institutional gaps, complex governance environments, diverse stakeholders, diverse relationships, networked governance structures, complex governance mechanisms, and the need for synergy between home and host countries and between parent and subsidiary companies. Therefore, studies of multinational corporate governance answer the questions of how to design effective corporate governance mechanisms and how to predict and avoid multinational corporate governance risks.

Four main theories explain the causes of corporate governance issues. Agency theory, the most widely accepted, plays a leading role in forming corporate governance mechanisms. The other three are the stewardship theory, stakeholder theory, and institutional theory.

3.1.1 Theories Related to Corporate Governance Studies

3.1.1.1 Agency Theory

Agency theory, proposed by Berle and Means (1932), is a fundamental theory of information economics. It investigates the optimal contractual arrangement under the condition of asymmetric information. The separation of ownership and control in modern companies leads to apparent information asymmetry about operating efficiency between company owners and managers, which creates a principal-agent relationship between shareholders (owners) and managers. Managers, as the agents, are at an advantage in obtaining a company's business information, whereas shareholders (owners), as the principals, are at a disadvantage in this regard once they are separated from the company's operations. A company is owned by its shareholders but controlled by its managers. Asymmetric information and incomplete contracts may lead to adverse selection and moral hazards, creating inconsistent goals between managers and shareholders. To address this problem, shareholders need to use a series of measures to motivate, supervise, and restrict managers to work as much as possible to maximise shareholder value.

Corporate governance emerges because of agency problems. Modern corporate governance studies focus on the relationship between shareholders and managers under the agency framework, aiming to find the optimal governance arrangements to maximise corporate value and prevent managers from damaging shareholders' interests in pursuit of personal interests. The ultimate goal of corporate governance is to solve agency and insider control problems resulting from the separation of ownership and control.

As researchers have investigated these issues in more depth, they have found that agency theory is limited because a company has a diverse group of stakeholders. For example, apart from owners and operators, employees, suppliers, consumers, and communities should also be considered in corporate governance. As a result, agency theory cannot account for the risks accruing to stakeholders other than owners and operators. In summary, the principal-agent relationship mainly leads to the following issues: majority shareholders damaging the interests of minority shareholders (also known as 'tunnelling'), shareholder representatives damaging the interests of shareholders, business risks arising from moral hazards and adverse selection, risks that shareholders face in providing incentives to management, and business risks due to inadequacies of the management.

3.1.1.2 Stewardship Theory

The development of Stewardship theory can be divided into two stages: classical stage and modern stage. Neoclassical economics assumes that companies are rational economic entities and that markets are perfectly competitive. The corresponding corporate governance theory is known as classical stewardship theory, according to which information and capital can flow freely in the market and companies are in perfect competition. Under the assumption of perfect information, business owners and business operators enter into a fiduciary relationship on a disinterested basis. Business operators never manage the business in a way that is against the owners' interests and always assign priority to these interests. Therefore, there is no agency problem. Because of the perfect information assumption, classical stewardship theory is inconsistent with reality. The actual conditions of imperfect information mean that this theory cannot explain the separation of the CEO and chairperson roles or the CEO duality found in modern companies, nor can it explain corporate governance behaviour in modern market conditions. As an early corporate governance theory, it is irrelevant for modern corporate governance studies.

Based on modern organisational theories and organisational behaviour research, Lex Donaldson (1990) put forward the modern stewardship theory, which diverges significantly from the agency theory. Donaldson argued that some assumptions of the agency theory, especially the assumption that business operators are opportunistic and lazy, are inappropriate. Instead, operators generally work hard to run a business and become good stewards of the business to pursue dignity, faith, and the intrinsic satisfaction obtained from doing a good job. In addition, modern stewardship theory emphasises that business operators under self-control have common interests with other related entities. However, in its reliance on the self-discipline of operators, this theory of corporate governance ignores the fact that operators are also self-interested economic actors. Thus, the theory attracts little attention now, as corporate democracy prevails, institutional investors dominate, and insider control and agency issues have a high profile.

3.1.1.3 Stakeholder Theory

Freeman's stakeholder theory (1984) holds that a company is a system composed of different providers of the factors of production (i.e., the company's stakeholders) and various factors drive that value creation. The purpose of a company is not only to maximise the interests of shareholders but also to create wealth and increase value for all stakeholders. This theory does not deny shareholder primacy, but emphasises a balance between shareholder and stakeholder interests. Accordingly, the goal of corporate governance is to maximise not only shareholder value but the total interests of all stakeholders. To achieve this goal, stakeholders should be allowed to share the ownership of a company and participate in corporate governance, the board of directors should be diverse, and stakeholders should have a say in the board of directors. In addition to shareholders, stakeholders may include employees, banks, major suppliers and customers, community representatives, and local governments.

Both classical stewardship theory and agency theory aim at maximising shareholder value. However, these theories have been increasingly criticised for excluding the interests of other stakeholders. Stakeholder theory expands corporate governance from the principal-agent relationship between company owners and operators to a systematic project of coordinating the relationship between internal management, internal stakeholders, external stakeholders, and other interest groups. It has dramatically broadened the scope of corporate governance and promoted the transformation of corporate governance concepts.

3.1.1.4 Institutional Theory

Ian Robertson (1987) pointed out that 'an institution is a stable cluster of values, norms, status, roles and groups that develops around a basic social need' and provides rigid patterns of thought and behaviour and proposes methods to solve recurring problems and satisfy social life needs. Douglass C. North (1990) defined institutions as the rules of the game in a society. He held that institutions consist of three parts: informal constraints widely accepted in society, formal rules stipulated by the state, and enforcement mechanisms. These three parts reinforce and restrict each other and jointly determine the implications and performance of an institution. From the perspective of institutional design, corporate governance is the organisational arrangement by which a company represents and serves the interests of its investors. It aims to reduce uncertainty from the formal and informal institutions, provide guidance, and confer legitimacy and rewards to managers and firms through different levels of structural design, from the executive incentive plans to the company's board arrangements. The need for corporate governance arises from the separation of ownership from control in modern joint-stock companies under a market economy. From a narrow perspective, corporate governance refers to institutional arrangements relating to the board's role and structure and the shareholder rights of a company. More broadly, it refers to a set of legal, cultural, and institutional arrangements intended for governing the allocation of a company's control rights or residual claims. These arrangements determine the company's objectives, who exercises control under what circumstances in what ways, and how risks and benefits are distributed between company members.

Corporate governance involves the relationship between a company's stakeholders and the goals for which the company is governed. As the agency chain extends during globalisation, a company takes on a more diversified group of stakeholders, and a host of new agency problems arise from the expansion of institutional boundaries. At the same time, existing corporate governance theories are challenged by a range of issues, such as various governance entities involved in various levels, including the home and host countries, the parent company and foreign subsidiaries. Differences in regulatory institutions, and complex governance environments and information processing. The traditional corporate governance experience is barely applicable to MNEs because of the complex governance environment and information asymmetry resulting from an institutional distance. Therefore, it is necessary to build a new theoretical model to analyse multinational corporate governance.

3.1.2 Theories Related to MNE Studies

Some of the major theories relating to multinational corporate governance are Hymer's monopolistic advantage theory, Vernon's product life cycle theory, Buckley's internalisation theory, and Dunning's eclectic paradigm of international production.

Hymer (1960) first put forward the monopolistic advantage theory in his 1960 doctoral dissertation, with an analysis at the micro-level. Later, the theory was improved by Kindleberger (1975) and Caves (1971), who argued that the spread of MNEs' advantages in the home country to host countries was the motive for multinational production. MNEs take advantage of product market imperfections to gain monopoly power in the home country through oligopolistic competition and collusion. When market expansion in the home country reaches a critical point, MNEs transfer their monopolistic or firm-specific advantages to foreign countries to replicate the monopoly position and profits they have achieved in the home country and ultimately create an oligopoly and collusive network in the global market. These firm-specific advantages include proprietary technologies, economies of scale, financial and monetary advantages, and organisational management capability. Caves (1971) developed the specific asset theory based on Hymer's theory, arguing that the advantage of an MNE lies in the synergy between its specific assets in the home country and its complementary assets in host countries. The monopolistic advantage theory suggests that a company with a monopolistic advantage in an imperfectly competitive market would directly invest in other countries to make the most of this advantage. It explains why MNEs carry out FDI and highlights the important role that intellectual assets and technological advantages play in FDI. The theory sparked new ideas in FDI studies and separated MNE theories from international trade and capital flow theories; however, it does not explain the reasons why companies with technological advantages invest abroad, the geographic distribution and location choice of foreign investment by MNEs, or the FDI behaviour of developing countries.

Vernon (1966) proposed the product life cycle theory to explain why US-based ('American') MNEs engage in FDI. This theory divides the life cycle of a product into three phases: innovation, maturation, and standardisation. As new product development is knowledge-intensive, the production and consumption of a new product often first appear in only a few developed countries with obvious technological advantages. These products are also exported to other wealthy countries. In the second phase, the production shifts from knowledge intensity to technology and capital intensity. Mass production requires machinery and skilled labour. Therefore, countries with sufficient capital and skilled workers have an advantage over the countries where the products were invented and gradually become the major producers and exporters. In the third phase, product technology is integrated into the equipment and production lines to standardise the production process and simplify operations. In this way, knowledge and technology can be transferred easily, product prices decrease, labour costs come to matter more than technology and capital, and thus production in knowledge-intensive countries and technology-

and capital-intensive countries becomes unprofitable. Therefore, production moves to countries with abundant labour resources, and products are exported to the initial producer countries.

Vernon's theory explains the motivation, timing, and location choice of FDI. Companies decide whether to make FDI based on the conditions of production and competitiveness. However, this theory is associated with the product market and does not apply to resource and technology development investments unrelated to the product life cycle. In addition, it can only explain the initial multinational investment of an MNE and fails to account for the investment behaviour of an MNE that has already established international production and sales systems.

The internalisation theory of Buckley and Casson (1976) is the first systematic study, whose core is Coase's firm theory (Coase, 1937) and Williamson's asset specificity theory (Williamson, 1975). It was proposed by Rugman (1980) as a general paradigm. The theory hypothesises that companies replace external markets to improve efficiency. Unlike the monopolistic advantage theory, the internalisation theory assumes that intermediate product markets, especially the technology market, are imperfectly competitive. According to this theory, MNEs result from cross-border market internalisation. They have emerged and developed to overcome externalities caused by government intervention and control. MNEs eliminate efficiency distortions caused by imperfect market competition by internalising intermediate product markets. The boundaries of an MNE are determined by when the external transaction costs equal the internal transaction costs. Following Coase's line of argument, the internalisation theory tries to prove that MNEs are the outcome of internalised activities that transcend national boundaries. As a vital turning point in Western studies on MNE theories, this theory analyses the organisational forms of the international division of labour and production and the nature and origin of MNEs. As a general theory of MNEs, it can explain the motives for most FDI and various business practices of MNEs.

The comparative advantage theory developed by Kojima (1973, 1978, 1982) explains the FDI behaviour of 'Japanese-type' MNEs. This theory analyses Japan's successful foreign investment from the international division of labour and comparative advantage perspectives. According to the theory, Japan succeeded because it moved sectors that were losing their advantages in the domestic market abroad while developing those with comparative advantages at home, thus creating a more substantial industrial structure.

According to the eclectic paradigm of international production proposed by Dunning (1977, 1979), a company engages in FDI because of the combined effect of three factors: ownership, internalisation, and location advantages. These are the necessary and sufficient conditions for a company to engage in FDI, and in combination, they determine whether a company undertakes export, licensing, or FDI. Therefore, they can comprehensively explain FDI and the behaviour of MNEs. The eclectic paradigm is a comprehensive and general theory of MNEs that integrates monopolistic advantage theory and internalisation theory. It establishes an analytic model based on three types of advantages that are indispensable for multinational operations: a company must have ownership, internalisation, and location advantages to engage in FDI activities.

Global sustainable competitive advantage theory analyses the resource positioning, resources and performance, strategic choice, and competitive advantage of MNEs from the perspective of resources rather than products. FDI path theory posits the interplay between the FDI behaviour of MNEs and the economic development of host countries. Resource determinism theory argues that MNEs are influenced by their dependence on local strategic assets and operating resources when choosing their equity ownership structures in overseas investment. The institutional theory highlights the significant impact of institutional factors on MNEs' choices of equity strategies. According to this theory, national risks, the host government's equity restrictions, and cultural differences are all important influences.

3.2 Characteristics of Multinational Corporate Governance

Multinational corporate governance has four major characteristics. First, due to an expanded group of stakeholders, multinational corporate governance is network governance in nature; second, the cascading extended agency chain complicates the corporate governance decision-making processes of MNEs; third, compared to corporate governance, multinational corporate governance involves a group of companies at home and abroad, rather than a single company, and covers internal and external governance; fourth, MNEs have to handle more diverse institutional elements and systems and more complicated coordination between governance mechanisms. Therefore, they need a unified governance culture to achieve organisational alignment.

3.2.1 Network Governance Attributes

The scale, scope, and influence of an MNE expand the potential stakeholders to include the host countries, home country, parent company, foreign subsidiaries, and partner companies. The dynamic interactions between the parent company, foreign subsidiaries, and other entities involved in corporate governance form a complex network. The parent company and a group of geographically dispersed subsidiaries constitute an internal network. The subsidiaries are embedded in the internal network; hence, their behaviour is under corresponding influence and constraint. At the same time, the subsidiaries can connect with local organisations in host countries (including customers, suppliers, and government agencies) to establish external network relationships, such as strategic alliances, joint ventures, and long-term relationships with external shareholders. Therefore, multinational corporate governance is, in essence, a type of network governance, and its characteristics make it different from both group governance and domestic corporate governance (Lin et al., 2009). In summary, compared with domestic companies, MNEs have an expanded group of stakeholders due to expanded corporate boundaries. MNEs need to balance the interests of all stakeholders by engaging in behaviour that goes beyond what can be explained by stakeholder theory.

3.2.2 Extended Agency Chain

The traditional corporate governance theory primarily studies the agency relationship between shareholders and managers. However, the multinational operation of an MNE exacerbates information asymmetry, causing agency problems between the parent company and its subsidiaries (Gupta & Govindarajan, 2000; Nohria & Ghoshal, 1994; Roth & O'Donnell, 1996). An MNE involves cascading principal-agent relationships at two levels. First, shareholders are the original principals, and members of management are the agents, as is the case in domestic companies. Second, the parent company, having set up foreign subsidiaries through FDI, is the direct principal, and the foreign subsidiaries are the agents. In addition, the parent company and foreign subsidiaries face major agency problems due to the information asymmetry resulting from the long distance between them. The cascading extended agency chain complicates the corporate governance decision-making process in MNEs.

Traditional corporate governance theory has focused primarily on dispersed share ownership systems and dealt with the agency relationship between the shareholders and management of a company (Song et al., 2010). However, as the organisational boundaries expand, the principal-agent relationship spans national borders, and the extended agency chain gives birth to a network of principal-agent relationships. In addition, the global expansion of foreign subsidiaries extends property relations and triggers changes in organisational form and the governance environment. Therefore, in an MNE, the principal-agent relationship goes beyond the scope of that in a single domestic business group. Because this relationship is expressed differently and involves more complex structural relations in MNEs, traditional agency theory cannot explain the related behaviour.

3.2.3 *Expanded Connotations of Internal and External Governance*

In MNEs, corporate governance involves multiple companies instead of a single one, which expands internal and external governance connotations. Internal governance mainly covers the parent company, foreign subsidiaries, and the relationship between them. Governance of the parent company focuses on the board size, ownership structure, and managerial incentives, whereas governance of foreign subsidiaries involves their boards of directors and senior management. Governance of the parent-subsidiary relationship revolves around the parent company's control over its subsidiaries and the equity governance of the subsidiaries. Compared with domestic companies, MNEs have expanded the scope of external governance to cover more issues, such as the influence of host country institutions, culture, and stakeholders.

3.2.4 *Cultural Dominance in Multinational Corporate Governance*

Due to differences in cultural background and business philosophy, decision-making style, decision constraints, and governance methods can differ significantly between a parent company and a subsidiary and across subsidiaries. In addition, cultural diversity is likely to cause internal divergence with a company regarding how to treat the government, employees, and other stakeholders. Facing more diverse institutional elements and environments and more complex coordination between governance mechanisms, MNEs need a unified and dominant governance culture.

In summary, multinational corporate governance shows different characteristics from traditional corporate governance. Consequently, mainstream corporate governance theories do not apply to multinational corporate governance and cannot explain the related behaviour.

3.3 Basic Theories and Framework for Multinational Corporate Governance

This section reviews and develops the abovementioned corporate governance theories, analyses the characteristics of multinational corporate governance, and provides a theoretical framework for multinational corporate governance based on stakeholder, agency, institutional design, decision-making, and network theories.

3.3.1 Stakeholder Theory

According to Wu (2008), the stakeholders of an MNE include the home country, the host countries, and international organisations at the macro-level; social groups, media, and the public in the place where the MNE is located at the meso-level; and member companies (the parent company and subsidiaries) and their shareholders, creditors, customers, suppliers, employees, labour unions, consumers, and the natural environment at the micro-level. The various stakeholders are shown in Fig. 3.1.

Stakeholders that can influence the governance of an MNE can be divided into external and internal stakeholders. The former group includes the government, social organisations, creditors, customers, and suppliers, and the latter includes shareholders, managers at all levels, and employees (Li, 2008).

In China, the government plays an important role in the operation of a Chinese MNE by supervising or supporting the company, especially in its entry into a foreign market. In countries with relatively large power distance, the government has a major influence on the operation and management of an MNE of its country, making it the most important external stakeholder. Social organisations, such as local labour unions, environmental protection organisations, and industry associations, are stakeholders of an MNE because they are affected by the MNE's business activities. Their relevance to an MNE depends on the laws of the country in which they are located and the degree of social responsibility that the MNE is willing to bear. An MNE is in a contractual relationship with its

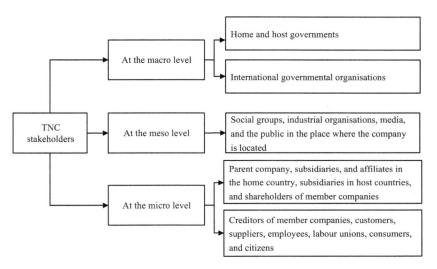

Fig. 3.1 Stakeholders of an MNE

creditors, whose relevance to the MNE depends on the relevant laws and social customs in the country in which they are located. The relevance between customers and an MNE depends on the product market, public opinion supervision, and legal protection in the country in which they are located.

The internal stakeholders of an MNE include the parent company and its subsidiaries in the home country and foreign subsidiaries and their affiliates in host countries. The different strategic roles of the subsidiaries lead to different parent-subsidiary relationships and thus give rise to different governance issues. Some of the directors, supervisors, and shareholders of an MNE are foreign institutional investors or individual investors; this phenomenon not only expands the range of stakeholders but also further differentiates the mutually beneficial connections with the MNE between shareholders. Top managers are undoubtedly the most important stakeholders of an MNE, as their business decisions determine the company's future. These managers are from different countries, and their attention to corporate governance varies due to cultural differences. MNEs usually hire local employees in host countries to avoid cross-border mobility. How much attention they pay to the multinational governance of the company depends on the economic institutions and legal environment in the host country.

To conclude, MNEs are at the centre of a series of multilateral relations, and their operation directly influences all interested individuals and groups. Therefore, while ensuring the interests of shareholders, MNEs must also consider the potential influence of their actions on employees, consumers, suppliers, communities, the environment, the home and host countries, and the international community.

3.3.2 Agency Theory

MNEs design their governance structure through M&As, splits, and sales of subsidiaries. As the ownership is broken down into fractional interests, MNEs become joint-stock companies that the parent company controls or has a stake in. Thus, MNEs feature agency relationships between shareholders and the parent company and between the parent company and subsidiaries. The multi-level agency system among the parent company, foreign subsidiaries, and group companies causes an overlap of multiple agency relationships (Song et al., 2010). Generally, an MNE has an agency chain like that shown in Fig. 3.2.

An MNE has a multi-level agency chain spanning from the parent company's initial agent to the operators of foreign subsidiaries; therefore, the agency relationship between the parent company and subsidiaries

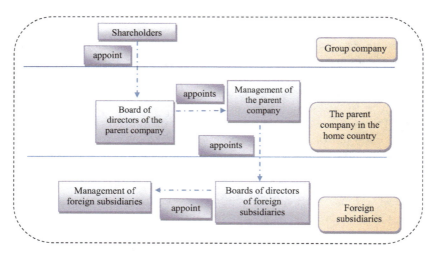

Fig. 3.2 Agency chain of an MNE

crosses national borders. Due to the long distance and the expanded agency chain, the initial principal cannot be expected to observe and control the operation of foreign subsidiaries directly and efficiently. In addition, the significant differences in business environments and corporate operating mechanisms make it complicated for them to conclude contracts. Therefore, the key to multinational corporate governance is to solve cross-border agency problems, and the solution to these problems is to ensure the effective functioning of the agency chain at all levels.

3.3.3   Institutional Design Theory

Over time, the governance systems of an MNE gradually form a multinational corporate governance culture. Due to different cultural backgrounds and business philosophies, the decision-making, decision constraints, and governance methods differ significantly between a parent company and a subsidiary and between subsidiaries. Board members from different countries think in different ways because of different cultural backgrounds and business habits. The efficiency and value of cross-cultural cooperation come from the entities in each culture that have advantages in local markets and the multicultural environment, inspiring creativity. Therefore, each MNE has a specific multinational corporate governance culture shaped by the cultures of different countries, and the subsidiaries inherit the parent company's culture. Thus, multinational corporate governance theory deals with the influences of the cultures mentioned above on multinational governance and the unique internal governance culture resulting from such influences.

An MNE needs an inclusive mechanism to give full play to the advantages of its constituent units with different cultural backgrounds and to pay full respect to each culture. The entities in an MNE must understand each other's business mindset, corporate culture, and social culture to communicate and work more efficiently and achieve win–win outcomes for all parties. For example, Lenovo adopted a parallel cultures model after acquiring IBM's PC business unit. The new company introduced a 'one company, two systems' policy to retain the advanced cultures of both Lenovo and IBM. The two cultures are allowed to retain their unique features and to remain independent of each other. Employees from the two cultures are encouraged to communicate and cooperate as much as possible and on a reasonable basis, complementing each other's advantages regardless of their differences.

3.3.4 Decision-Making Theory

An MNE usually has a complete decision-making system and an identified highest decision-making centre. Each subsidiary has its own decision-making body that makes decisions according to its different features and operations, but its decisions must be subordinated to the highest decision-making centre. In an MNE with an ethnocentric orientation, decision-making serves the interests of the home country and the parent company. The parent company makes most of the management decisions and adopts centralised management of foreign subsidiaries. This decision-making system emphasises the consistency of corporate goals. It can give full play to the parent company's central role in adjusting optimal resources use. However, such a system erodes the autonomy and initiative of subsidiaries and is unpopular in host countries. In an MNE with a polycentric orientation, decision-making tends to serve the interests of host countries and foreign subsidiaries. The parent company allows subsidiaries to independently determine business objectives and long-term development strategies based on country-specific conditions. The parent company devolves decision-making power to subsidiaries and adopts a decentralised management system. This mechanism emphasises flexible and adaptable management styles that enhance the initiative and sense of responsibility of subsidiaries. This approach is well received in host countries. In an MNE with a monocentric orientation, the decision-making aims to maximise the company's global interests. Accordingly, the company adopts a combined management system which puts the overall decision and management power in the hands of the parent company. It allows foreign subsidiaries to make action plans and allocate and use resources in line with the parent company's overall business strategy. As a result, subsidiaries enjoy significant autonomy in business operations. This decision-making mechanism gives each subsidiary a certain degree of autonomy while maintaining the company's global business objectives and can thus boost the initiative and enthusiasm of subsidiaries.

In summary, unlike the domestic companies, MNEs must think globally and stay vigilant in the uncertain global business environment when making strategic decisions (e.g., where to set up a subsidiary, how to set up the subsidiary, and which equity mode of entry to use), management decisions (e.g., what operating tasks the parent company should complete in a certain period, and how to balance the interests of operating entities), and executive decisions (such as decisions made by the company's operating entities, especially foreign subsidiaries, in line with the parent company's overall deployment). They need to consider more diverse and complex factors and follow different guidelines, methods, procedures, and mechanisms. Based on group decision-making theory, the decision-making by MNEs is generally considered a behavioural outcome of collective ideas and business operations experience.

3.3.5 Network Governance Theory

MNEs are networks of related enterprises. They are composed of a parent company and foreign subsidiaries or affiliates that form an internal network based on ownership connections, cooperation, and information sharing. An MNE network involves an ownership network, the transfer of managers, and related transaction networks and is an inter-organisational network (Ghoshal & Bartlett, 1990). The foreign subsidiaries of an MNE are embedded in two different networks: an internal network consisting of the parent company and foreign subsidiaries, and an external network consisting of the MNE and its market and social relations in the host countries in which the subsidiaries are located (Andersson & Forsgren, 1995). As an MNE sets up overseas branches worldwide during multinational operations, an internal network is formed based on the ownership connections, cooperation, and information sharing between the headquarters and branches. Operating across national borders, MNEs face not only a complex and uncertain institutional environment but also new and highly uncertain industrial ecosystems in host countries. It is particularly time-consuming and challenging for MNEs from emerging markets or developing countries to be recognised and accepted by the governments, industrial organisations, and consumers in host countries (Xue & Li, 2011). For this to occur, they need to connect with local stakeholders, thus forming an external network (Fig. 3.3).

According to Lin et al. (2009) and Wu and Huang (2010), multinational enterprise groups have a specific internal network in which their subsidiaries are embedded. The internal network can facilitate message passing and resource sharing between the subsidiaries and agencies, thereby helping them make and improve strategic plans. It can also provide foreign subsidiaries with key resources needed for development and help them overcome outsider defects in host countries (Andersson et al., 2002). Nohria and Ghoshal (1997) pointed out that the branches and subsidiaries of an MNE can share network resources to a certain

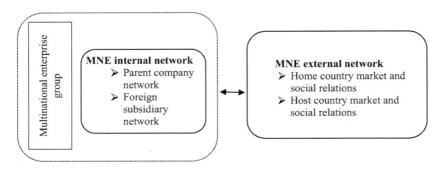

Fig. 3.3 Network structures in which the foreign subsidiaries of MNEs are embedded

extent. A foreign subsidiary can draw on other subsidiaries' experiences and lessons to develop its strategies more efficiently. Foreign subsidiaries of the same parent company can establish close ties and make frequent exchanges to obtain the information and resources they need to tackle challenges in the parent company's home country and the host countries.

MNEs connect with local organisations through external cooperation networks, which can not only serve as channels of information and resource exchange but also improve their legitimacy. Foreign subsidiaries embedded in specific social networks can fit in more quickly with the host country environment, obtain better reviews from stakeholders, obtain necessary information, and improve their learning abilities and adaptability through online learning, feedback, and influence mechanisms (Xue & Hou, 2005). Lin et al. (2009) studied China's TD-SCDMA-based 3G industry and pointed out that Chinese subsidiaries of MNEs from developed countries can improve their local legitimacy by establishing connections with indigenous companies.

Thus, MNEs can create internal sub-networks between their branches and subsidiaries in the same country to promote information flow and sharing among these subsidiaries and improve their operating performance. They can also obtain the information they need, improve their learning abilities and adaptability, and gain local legitimacy by building external cooperation networks.

In summary, the theoretical framework for multinational corporate governance consists of five basic theories: stakeholder theory, agency theory, institutional design theory, decision-making theory, and network theory.

References

Andersson, U., & Forsgren, M. (1995). Subsidiary embeddedness and control in the multinational corporation. *International Business Review, 5*(5), 487–508.

Andersson, U., Forsgren, M., & Holm, U. (2002). The strategic impact of external networks: Subsidiary performance and competence development in the multinational corporation. *Strategic Management Journal, 23*(11), 979–996.

Berle, A., & Means, G. (1932). *The modern corporation and private property*. Macmillan.

Buckley, P. J., & Casson, M. (1976). *The future of the multinational enterprise*. Holmes and Meier.

Caves, R. (1971). International corporations: The industrial economics of foreign investment. *Economica, 38*, 1–27.

Kindleberger, C. P. (1975). Monopolistic theory of direct foreign investment. *International Political Economy*.

Coase, R. H. (1937). The nature of firm. *Economica, 4*(16), 386–405.

Donaldson, L. (1990). The ethereal hand: Organizational economics and management theory. *The Academy of Management Review, 15*(3), 369–381.

Dunning, J. H. (1977). Trade, location of economic activity and the MNE: A search for an eclectic approach. *The International Allocation of Economic Activity*.

Dunning, J. H. (1979). Explaining changing patterns of international production. In Defence of the Eclectic Theory. *Oxford Bulletin of Economics and Statistics, 41*, 269–295.

Ghoshal, S., & Bartlett, C. (1990). The multinational corporation as an interorganizational network. *The Academy of Management Review, 15*, 603–635.

Gupta, A. K., & Govindarajan, V. (2000). Knowledge flows within multinational corporations. *Strategic Management Journal, 21*(4), 473–496.

Hymer, S. H. (1960). *The international operation of national firms: A study of direct foreign investment*. Doctoral dissertation, Massachusetts Institute of Technology.

Li, X. D. (2008). *An Analysis and Evaluation of Corporate Governance of Multinational Corporations*. Harbin Engineering University Press.

Lin, R. H., Zhang, H. J., Fan, J. H., & Shuai, Y. X. (2009). Evaluation research on group enterprise network governance—A case study of Acer. *Corporate Governance Review, 1*(04), 29–44.

Kojima, K. (1973). A macroeconomic approach to foreign direct investment. *Hitotsubashi Journal of Economics, 14*(1), 1–21.

Kojima, K. (1978). *Direct foreign investment: A Japanese model of multinational business operations.* Croom Helm.

Kojima, K. (1982). Macroeconomic versus international business approach to direct foreign investment. *Hitotsubashi Journal of Economics, 23*(1), 1–19.

Nohria, N., & Ghoshal, S. (1994). Differentiated fit and shared values: Alternatives for managing headquarters–subsidiary relations. *Strategic Management Journal, 15*(6), 491–502.

Nohria, N., & Ghoshal, S. (1997). *The differentiated network: Organising multinational corporations for value creation.* Jossey-Bass Publishers.

North, D. C. (1990). *Institutions, institutional change, and economic performance.* Harvard University Press.

Robertson, I. (1987). *Sociology.* Worth Publishers press. Chapters 13–18.

Roth, K., & O'Donnell, S. (1996). Foreign subsidiary compensation strategy: An agency theory perspective. *Academy of Management Journal, 39*(3), 678–703.

Rugman, A. M. (1980). Internalization theory and corporate international finance. *California Management Review, 23*(2), 73–79.

Song, G. H., Wang, X. H., & Qin, Q. D. (2010). Corporate governance of foreign subsidiaries of state-run multinational corporations—From a perspective of dual or multiple overlapping agency relationships. *Journal of Finance and Economics, 36*(11), 62–71.

Vernon, R. (1966). International investment and international trade in the product cycle. *The Quarterly Journal of Economics, 80*(2), 190–207.

Williamson, E. (1975). *Markets and hierarchies: Analysis and antitrust implications, a study in the economics of internal organisation [M].* New York: Free Press.

Wu, G. Y. (2008). Enhancing the social responsibility of multinational corporations from the perspective of stakeholder cooperation. *Journal of Guangxi Economic Management Cadre College, 2008*(2), 13–21.

Wu, L. D., & Huang, H. X. (2010). Subsidiary initiative and embeddedness of enterprise groups internal network: A case study of hisense group [J]. *Nankai Business Review, 13*(06), 125–137.

Xue, Q., & Hou, S. (2005). The research on positioning models of overseas subsidiaries: A transition of the angle of view from headquarters to subsidiaries. *Nankai Business Review, 8*(4), 60–66.

Xue, Q., & Li, Q. Q. (2011). Legitimation process of chinese multinational corporations—Based on the population density dependent model. *World Economy Studies, 2011*(3), 63–89.

CHAPTER 4

Multinational Corporate Governance: A Network Governance Framework

Research on multinational corporate governance is proliferating within and outside of China, mainly considering behaviour and cognition from the perspectives of the agency theory, resource-based theory, institutional theory, the integration of agency theory and resource dependence theory, and social capital and network theory. This research has covered a wide range of areas and generated numerous findings. The topic has been explored from various perspectives in the literature, and studies differ significantly within and outside of China. Li et al. (2011) and Denis and McConnell (2003) divided corporate governance into internal and external governance. The former primarily focuses on board size, ownership structure, and managerial incentives, whereas the latter mainly relates to government regulations and laws. Zhou et al. (2008) conducted a literature review on MNE corporate governance based on research findings from the outside-in, inside-out, and combined inside/outside perspectives.

However, these studies have failed to identify the unique characteristics of multinational corporate governance: a long governance chain, a large group of stakeholders, and the involvement of diverse institutions and cultures. Therefore, a research framework based on internal and external thinking cannot adequately account for multinational corporate governance. Furthermore, previous research has not considered that MNEs, as network organisations, are embedded in external networks

© The Author(s), under exclusive license to Springer Nature Singapore Pte Ltd. 2022
R. Lin and J. J. Chen, *The Theory and Application of Multinational Corporate Governance*, https://doi.org/10.1007/978-981-16-7703-8_4

composed of customers, suppliers, and governments. In such a network, different business units in an MNE need to interact with each other. Therefore, the scope of multinational corporate governance should be expanded to include the dynamic interaction between the home country, host countries, and MNEs (Alpay et al., 2005; Luo, 2005).

The main difference between an MNE and a single company is that an MNE consists of a parent company and a group of geographically dispersed subsidiaries, forming an inter-organisational network (Ghoshal & Bartlett, 1990). The behaviours of these subsidiaries are affected and constrained by their internal network embeddedness. An MNE includes formal and informal network relationships. Formal relationships enable workforce mobility, resource exchange, and personnel transfer within an MNE's internal network (Nohria & Ghoshal, 1997). Informal relationships refer to relations between people, such as friendships and internal network interactions within an MNE (Kilduff & Tsai, 2003). Subsidiaries can connect with local organisations (such as customers, suppliers, and government agencies) in host countries to establish external network relationships (Andersson & Forsgren, 1996). A closely connected network within an MNE can help develop competitive advantages, thereby enhancing its competitiveness (Ghoshal & Bartlett, 1990). Individual subsidiaries establish external network relationships, such as strategic alliances, joint ventures, and long-term relationships with external shareholders. With these network relationships, subsidiaries can learn new knowledge and obtain the necessary information, resources, markets, or technologies to achieve their goals (such as risk diversification and outsourcing) and reduce speculation.

Multinational business group governance is essentially a form of network governance (Zaheer et al., 2000) that involves a complex network consisting of a parent company, subsidiaries, and other entities. It is different from group governance in the general sense because foreign subsidiaries play different strategic roles in a multinational context. These different strategic roles lead to different parent-subsidiary relationships that give rise to many governance issues. The strategic tasks of a foreign subsidiary should be accompanied by appropriate governance mechanisms, the presence of which is a key precondition for MNEs to achieve their desired organisational performance. Therefore, an MNE should adjust its multinational governance mechanisms to suit the different strategic roles played by its subsidiaries. Unlike previous studies, this chapter provides a literature review of multinational governance research findings from the perspective of network governance to reflect the complexity and unique characteristics of multinational corporate governance.

This chapter is structured as follows: the first part discusses the governance of the key nodes (i.e., the parent company and foreign subsidiaries) in an MNE as a network organisation. The second part covers the governance of the parent-subsidiary relationships within an MNE, and the final part analyses the external governance issues of an MNE.

4.1 MNE Network Node Governance

From the perspective of network governance, multinational corporate governance involves both the internal and external networks of MNEs. In an MNE, network governance refers to the governance of its network nodes: the parent company and its foreign subsidiaries.

4.1.1 Parent Company Governance

4.1.1.1 Governance of the Parent company's Board of Directors

Generally, strategic decisions on foreign investment of an MNE are made by the parent company's board of directors. Most scholars in China and abroad use upper echelons theory to explain board composition and characteristics, corporate globalisation strategies, and performance issues. This theory proposes that board characteristics greatly influence MNEs' strategic decision-making and performance (Finkelstein & Hambrick, 1996). Scholars have found that the board size and independent directors influence the foreign investment projects of an MNE (Lien et al., 2005), and the proportion of outside directors also affects the global performance of an MNE (Lu et al., 2009). Rivas (2012) found that corporate globalisation is positively related to the diversity of boards and management teams, longer management tenure, and younger board age.

These studies have primarily focused on MNEs in developed economies. Many of the findings relate to the influence of board composition on the strategic choices (such as M&As, diversification, and greenfield investment) of MNEs in developed economies because they started earlier than those in other economies. Lien et al. (2005) studied the influence of board size and independent directors on MNEs' foreign investment projects in Taiwan. Clark and Brown (2014) proposed four types of MNE boards in global business management: traditionalist, conformist, satisficing, and integrative. They offered suggestions on creating an integrated governance structure in MNEs and considered governance mechanisms, governance structures, and behaviours for improving the governance of MNEs. In a case study of nine MNEs in four Nordic countries, Piekkari et al. (2015) found that board members usually remained silent and rarely had discussions in board meetings when English was not used as a working language. Some board members found it difficult to contribute to board meetings and articulate disagreement. In contrast, such effects were not revealed in the well-prepared companies.

Relatively few studies have been conducted on the governance of TNCs in emerging economies. In a study based on the data of private companies in Russia, Ukraine, and Belarus, Filatotchev et al. (2001) found that management ownership had a negative effect on the adoption of export strategies and a positive effect on deterring exports inhibition of export-oriented product development. In the Chinese context, Lu et al. (2009) found that CEOs and the proportion of outside directors had positive effects on export intensity and the performance of enterprises. Based on analysis of 2006–2008 data on the influence of board attributes on the globalisation of listed companies in China, Zhou et al. (2013) found that the board of directors could improve a company's global operations and management and thereby accelerate its globalisation by absorbing more globalisation knowledge and internal information and by spending more time on team activities.

In short, when expanding their global business, MNEs increase the board size of the parent company, set up professional committees and subsidiary boards, and raise the proportion of outside directors in the boards of the parent company and its subsidiaries. When improving local responsiveness, they increase the board size of the parent company, raise the proportion of outside directors in subsidiaries, and give subsidiary boards greater autonomy and independence. As MNEs continue to accumulate global business experience, the boards of directors and management teams see greater diversity, and the parent company holds fewer stocks (Alpay et al., 2005).

4.1.1.2 Parent Company Equity Governance

Equity control was a major issue in early studies of multinational corporate governance (Brouthers & Hennart, 2007; Demirbag et al., 2009; Luo & Tung, 2007). Chan and Makino (2007) proposed that ownership is equivalent to a resource commitment made by a parent company to its subsidiaries. It is the result of cooperative negotiations between MNEs and host governments or local organisations and reflects the comparative bargaining power of the parties (Gomes-Casseres, 1990). Ownership is also equivalent to the parent company's degree of control over foreign subsidiaries' operations and strategic decisions (Hill et al., 1990).

Subsidiaries in MNEs are divided into three types: wholly owned, controlled, and non-controlled. Parent companies have greater control over the first two types. Facing environmental and market uncertainties during cross-border operations, MNEs need to cooperate with host country partners and establish controlled or non-controlled subsidiaries to improve their adaptability and legitimacy and gain competitive advantages. Hence, many studies on multinational corporate governance are centred on the equity governance models that MNEs have adopted when entering foreign markets. Most related studies have examined the topic through the lenses of transaction cost theory, institutional theory, political perspective, and upper echelons theory.

In an early study based on transaction cost theory, Anderson and Gatignon (1986) suggested that the most efficient entry mode strikes a balance between control and the costs of resource inputs. The three factors determining the optimal level of control are internal uncertainty, external uncertainty, and transaction specificity. With larger ownership stakes, more resource inputs, and higher input costs, MNEs have more controlling power. As transaction costs increase, MNEs may prefer to wholly own a subsidiary (Erramilli & Rao, 1993) to reduce transaction risks.

Unlike transaction cost theory, which emphasises efficiency, the institutional theory focuses on the legitimacy problems of foreign subsidiaries caused by the outsider and new entrant disadvantages when explaining the entry mode choices of MNEs (Kostova & Roth, 2002; Xu & Shenkar, 2002). Each foreign subsidiary is confronted with two distinct sets of isomorphic pressures and a need to maintain legitimacy within both the host country and the MNE. Such institutional duality affects cross-border governance (Kostova et al., 2008). To help foreign subsidiaries gain external legitimacy in host countries (Kostova & Zaheer, 1999), MNEs usually choose lower levels of control and resource inputs, and they share ownership with local partner companies in host countries. The empirical research confirms this view carried out by Chen et al. (2009) on the transitional economy of China. However, further research is still needed to see whether the cognition of institutional or cultural distance affects the entry mode choice and the performance of the chosen mode, and the influence of the interaction between institutional factors and other standards of decision-making on the final decision (Brouthers & Hennart, 2007).

Recent studies have explored the equity issues related to the foreign investment of MNEs from emerging economies through the lenses of political connections and upper echelons theory. For example, Cui and Jiang (2012) studied the influence of state-owned equity on Chinese companies' equity decisions in foreign investment. They expanded the application of institutional theory in international business research from a political perspective by arguing that when entering a foreign market, a company responds to external institutions differently if it has the political attributes of the external institutions. They held that government equity adds the political attributes of the home government to an MNE, increases its resource dependency on home country institutions, and affects the host government's impression of the MNE. Empirical studies have found that home country control, host country control, and host country regulatory pressures strongly influence companies, driving them to choose a joint venture structure when state-owned companies hold a relatively high proportion of shares. Based on upper echelons theory, Xie (2014) used a sample of Chinese listed companies to investigate the influence of CEO tenure on the equity model choices of Chinese MNEs investing abroad. According to the research results, CEO tenure was positively associated with choosing a total control model, and CEO duality could strengthen this association, but firm size and age had no apparent influence on such choices. Chen (2011) found that the positive relationship between top management tenure and a company's international experience was reinforced with a higher number of independent directors. This finding supports the view that independent directors as supervisors and resource providers can provide better advice to executives, enhancing their strategic action capabilities in their internationalisation efforts.

4.1.1.3 Governance of Parent Company Executives
Studies on the governance of executives cover executive background characteristics, MNE strategies, managerial incentive and restraint mechanisms, and executives' social networks and interactions with other managerial teams. Generally, research has focused on executive characteristics, MNE strategies, and executive remuneration.

Looking first at the issues related to executive characteristics and MNE strategies, according to upper echelons theory, a company reflects its top managers (Hambrick & Mason, 1984). The observable background characteristics of executives are valid proxies for their cognitive orientation, values, and knowledge base, which may significantly influence their decision-making (Herrmann & Datta, 2005). Strategic decisions are often made and implemented in dynamic processes through which managers interact, consult, and debate (Kor, 2006). Globalisation is a complex and costly process that requires all top managers' participation, support, and cooperation. Thus, the governance of top managers is critical to the implementation of the corporate strategies of MNEs, especially globalisation strategies. Scholars have investigated various factors, such as top management tenure, international experience, age profile, and nationality, on MNEs' globalisation strategies. These studies have primarily focused on MNEs in either developed or emerging economies.

In developed economies, Sambharya (1996) found a positive correlation between the international experience of top managers and their international involvement, suggesting that top managers with richer international experience are more likely to commit resources to global expansion and better manage and control multinational operations. Nielsen and Nielsen (2013) integrated upper echelons theory into the framework of institutional theory and investigated the relationship between an MNE's executive team and its performance. They found that the nationality diversity of the top management team (TMT) was positively related to firm performance and that this relation was enhanced under the conditions of (1) long management tenure, (2) a high degree of internationalisation, and (3) a liberal environment.

In emerging economies, Lu et al. (2014) investigated the internationalisation of Chinese companies and found that top managers' international experience could enhance the influence of domestic diversification on international diversification, whereas their previous political connections weakened such influence. Chen (2011) analysed a dataset of listed companies in Taiwan based on the upper echelons and agency theories and found that top management tenure was positively related to a company's international experience. In contrast, top management age was negatively correlated with the company's international experience. This finding supports the upper echelons theory.

Studies of multinational corporate governance have systematically investigated the impact of the executive compensation structure on organisational strategies, such as those associated with internationalisation. Sanders and Carpenter (1998) found that CEO compensation and long-term incentives were positively related to the degree of internationalisation of a company. Carpenter and Sanders (2004) found that the effect of executive pay increased with the degree of internationalisation of an MNE. Using the complementary lenses of information-processing and agency theories, Sanders and Carpenter (1998) tested the proposition that the complexity resulting from a high degree of internationalisation would be accommodated by a firm's governance structure. They used American companies as a research sample. Their research revealed that companies could meet the information-processing demands and solve the agency issues arising from internationalisation by offering high CEO pay and long-term incentives, employing a large executive team, and splitting the chairperson and CEO roles.

Recent studies have focused on the relationship between executive pay and behaviour and a company's global strategy. For example, McDonald et al. (2008) incorporated insights from social networks research into an agency theory perspective to investigate how governance factors influence CEOs' external advice-seeking behaviour. Using a conceptual framework that included high-level CEO equity ownership and performance-dependent compensation, they found that under the supervision of the board of directors, the CEO was more willing to seek advice from employees at other companies with whom they did not share a friendship or common functional backgrounds. The pay disparity between the CEO and top management team members is an important factor that influences the pace of internationalisation. From an economic perspective, a large pay gap drives managers to keep a regular pace. However, too large a pay gap may hinder cooperation between top managers and damage the pace of internationalisation from an equity perspective. Therefore, to ensure an appropriate pace of internationalisation, the compensation committee should consider the most appropriate pay gap between the CEO and top management team members. A large pay gap can prompt the top management team to collect foreign information and explore new foreign markets, but once the pay gap rises to a certain point, it may have a negative effect on the pace of internationalisation, mainly due to the lack of cooperation between top management members.

4.1.2 Foreign Subsidiary Governance

An MNE's subsidiaries are the key nodes in its internal governance network, especially those in the host countries, and play different strategic roles. A foreign subsidiary is embedded in a network composed of the host government, non-profit organisations, customers, and suppliers and needs to maintain its relationships with other subsidiaries. It is also subject to the influence of the parent company and the home government. Therefore, subsidiary governance in MNEs involves issues related to both single corporation governance and network governance. A key issue facing subsidiaries is allocating resources in such network organisations to facilitate more efficient and rational decision-making.

Each foreign subsidiary undertakes a unique task or role in the host country in which it is operated, and its activities are limited or determined by the country-specific task environment. A sound governance structure and sound governance mechanisms are important for dealing with the uncertain and complex environment in the host country. Foreign subsidiary governance has been a long-standing research topic of scholars in China and abroad. In view of the important strategic role of subsidiaries in MNEs' network governance, this section discusses three aspects of subsidiary governance: board governance, equity governance, and top management governance.

4.1.2.1 Governance of Subsidiary Boards of Directors

Important for internal governance and local resource acquisition, a subsidiary board performs four primary roles: control, strategic planning, coordination, and service (Alpay et al., 2005). The control role mainly involves supervising and approving important decisions made at the subsidiary level and evaluating subsidiary performance and management (Du et al., 2015; Reuer et al., 2014). The strategic planning role is similar to the decision-making function of the board of directors in a single company. The subsidiary board participates in the strategic planning of the subsidiary, identifies its strategic direction, and evaluates its strategic plan (Kiel et al., 2006; Kriger, 1988). The coordination role refers to transferring information and knowledge between the headquarters and the subsidiary (Leksell & Lindgren, 1982; Reuer et al., 2014). The service role mainly involves providing localised knowledge for the subsidiary's management team and communicating with local stakeholders so that the subsidiary can easily obtain local resources (Alpay et al., 2005). Many scholars have investigated how foreign subsidiary boards can improve the decision-making efficiency of foreign subsidiaries from various perspectives.

Early studies focused on the role of foreign subsidiary boards. An MNE's foreign subsidiaries usually face a highly uncertain environment. Subsidiary boards can reduce environmental uncertainties in host countries and help foreign subsidiaries respond flexibly to external environment changes. The role of foreign subsidiary boards is different from that of boards in single-member companies. First, in MNEs, agency problems arise when subsidiaries pursue different goals from those of the parent company (Jensen & Meckling, 1976; Meyer et al., 1992). A subsidiary board supervises the subsidiary's management performance to ensure its strategic decisions align with the MNE's overall goals, thereby reducing agency problems. In addition, as a bridge between the headquarters and subsidiaries, subsidiary boards can reduce information asymmetry between the headquarters and subsidiaries and facilitate the integration of subsidiaries into the MNE. Second, embedded in local networks, foreign subsidiaries rely on local stakeholders (such as customers, suppliers, and management agencies) to obtain important resources (Cantwell, 2009). Subsidiary boards establish contact with local stakeholders, reducing the dependence of foreign subsidiaries on local resources. Third, board directors of foreign subsidiaries become the protectors of the principal's interests, for which board composition is a key factor. Although inside directors have expertise in corporate decision-making, they cannot objectively evaluate the strategic decision-making process due to the influence of the CEO. However, outside directors lack corporate-specific knowledge and cannot understand the complexity of the corporate business. Donaldson and Davis (1994) found that having a high proportion of inside directors could help foreign subsidiaries make rapid decisions, thereby improving their performance.

In foreign subsidiary governance, the board of directors not only plays a supervisory role but also serves as a strategic governance mechanism. The unique knowledge of foreign subsidiaries is a source of competitive advantage for MNEs (Gupta & Govindarajan, 2000; Monteiro et al., 2008). Scholars have used different methods to describe the role of subsidiaries in the context of the conflicting needs of global integration and local response. For example, Birkinshaw and Morrison (1995) proposed three subsidiary role types: local implementer, specialised contributor, and world mandate. Subsidiaries operating as local implementers run only in local markets, carry out specific value-added activities, and are independent of other subsidiaries in an MNE. In contrast, subsidiaries operating as world mandates are responsible for a wide range of value-added activities and serve as part of the headquarters' development and implementation strategy. Subsidiaries operating as specialised contributors perform routine tasks and are well integrated into the multinational operations of an MNE. Du et al. (2011) found that a foreign subsidiary was more likely to maintain an active board of directors if it served as a world mandate with greater relevance to the parent company, a higher level of local response, and poorer past performance. Reuer et al. (2014) found that board involvement tended to reflect efficiency considerations in individual ventures and that the administrative control provided by boards was an important dimension of international joint venture governance.

4.1.2.2 Foreign Subsidiary Ownership Governance
The choice of foreign subsidiary ownership models, mainly between two types of ownership structures (whole ownership and shared ownership), is determined by such factors as trade-offs and resource commitments, level of control, and risk and return specificity (Cho et al., 2014). Gomes-Casseres (1989) paid early attention to the governance of foreign subsidiary ownership structures. In a study on MNEs' choices of their subsidiaries' equity ownership structure, he found that MNEs tended to prefer joint ventures over wholly owned subsidiaries in cases in which (1) the capabilities of the local firm complemented those of the MNE, (2) cooperation through contractual means was more expensive than equity cooperation, and (3) joint ventures would generate greater profits than other means.

From the perspective of corporate governance, Musteen et al. (2009) held that the purpose of ownership structure is to control opportunistic behaviours on the part of foreign subsidiary managers (such as institutional ownership and internal managerial ownership) and that the incentive mechanism should meet the interests of managers and shareholders. In a study of Japanese subsidiaries worldwide through the lenses of institutional theory and organisational theory, Gaur and Lu (2007) examined the main effects of ownership, institutional distance, and host country experience on the survival of subsidiaries. In a country with a greater institutional distance from the home country, subsidiaries had a greater chance of survival if the parent company had a larger stake in the subsidiary. Host country experience had a negative effect on subsidiary survival, but this effect was weaker if the parent company had a larger stake in the subsidiary. Cui and Jiang (2012) found that home country control, host country control, and host country regulatory pressures had a strong influence on Chinese companies, driving those for which the government had high stock ownership levels to choose joint venture ownership structures.

4.1.2.3 Foreign Subsidiary Top Management Governance

The strategic role of a foreign subsidiary affects its institutional arrangement of managerial incentives. For example, Roth and O'Donnell (1996) divided subsidiary strategic roles into global rationalisation (similar to specialised contributors) and horizontal centralisation (similar to world mandates). Compared with global rationalisation, horizontal centralisation requires subsidiary management to have more specialised knowledge and greater decision-making power and increases parent-subsidiary agency problems due to information asymmetry. O'Donnell (2000) held that horizontal centralisation aggravates the information asymmetry between parent and subsidiary companies and increases the difficulty and cost of supervising subsidiaries' management behaviour and decision-making. Research has shown that horizontal centralisation increases the interdependence of the parent and subsidiary, resulting in a higher level of non-monetary incentives related to career development.

The executive background characteristics of a foreign subsidiary affect its corporate performance. Drawing on a knowledge-based view and upper echelons theory, Sekiguchi et al. (2011) examined the influence of executive nationality on foreign subsidiary performance by analysing 643 Japanese subsidiaries of MNEs from 31 different countries. They found that top managers from the host country outperformed expatriate managers from the parent company in managing local employees and gaining legitimacy. The foreign subsidiaries ran for a longer period, but expatriate managers outshone local managers in the initial stage of the foreign subsidiaries' operations. Foreign subsidiaries with a larger-scale and shorter operation time performed better if they had a higher proportion of expatriate managers. This conclusion is consistent with Gong's research findings. In a study of foreign subsidiary managers of Japanese MNEs from the perspective of knowledge and legitimacy, Gong (2006) found that the nationality heterogeneity of the top management team was positively related to the company productivity and that heterogeneity thus had an increasing influence on subsidiary performance over time.

Fey and Furu (2008) explored the influence of foreign subsidiary executive pay and incentive mechanisms on the knowledge flow within MNEs. In a study of 164 overseas subsidiaries located in Finland and China, they sought to identify the relationship between subsidiary bonuses based on company-wide performance and knowledge sharing between different subsidiaries of MNEs. The result shows that incentive compensation based on the overall performance of an MNE boosted internal knowledge sharing. This suggests that the compensation system of an MNE can stimulate the flow of knowledge within the MNE, thereby exerting a positive influence on knowledge sharing within the corporation. The study also found that formal mechanisms, such as a performance-based compensation system, were important ways to encourage knowledge transfer, and the standard integration of subsidiaries into an MNE had a positive impact on sharing behaviours within the MNE.

4.2 MNEs Network Relationship Governance: Parent-Subsidiary Relationship Governance

Different subsidiary roles result in different parent-subsidiary relationships, leading to varying governance issues. A governance mechanism appropriate for a foreign subsidiary's strategic task is a critical context-specific condition for MNEs to achieve their desired organisational performance. Generally, MNEs choose the corporate governance mechanisms based on the agency problems present in the parent-subsidiary relationships. Therefore, multinational governance mechanisms should be adjusted to the different strategic roles of subsidiaries.

4.2.1 Parent Company Strategy and Parent-Subsidiary Governance

The research into parent-subsidiary relationships has been mainly associated with the subsidiary mandate frameworks (Roth & Morrison, 1992) and has suggested that MNEs establish subsidiaries with various strategic mandates. As such, the parent company's objectives have a dominant influence on a subsidiary's operations, decision-making processes, and strategy within the MNE's global production network, with the subsidiary acquiring or developing unique resources and capabilities to fulfil its mandate (Filatotchev et al., 2008). Moreover, when a foreign subsidiary is established through the full or partial acquisition of a local firm, its existing dynamic capabilities and knowledge may enable it to identify new market opportunities and thus more effectively achieve its mandate.

There are three types of subsidiary roles: local implementer, specialised contributor, and world mandate. The world mandate subsidiary is more freestanding than its local implementer or strategic contributor counterparts. It does not rely on lateral product flows to anything like the same extent, preferring instead to source its raw materials and sell its products externally. In terms of parent-subsidiary relationships, the strategic autonomy (a negative indicator of bureaucratic control) is highest in world mandate subsidiaries, so the world mandate type having the highest autonomy (Birkinshaw & Morrison, 1995). Based on the integration-response analysis framework, Kim et al. (2005) built a foreign subsidiary governance framework in which parent-subsidiary relationships are mainly affected by host country institutional environments and subsidiary capabilities. These two factors also influence the three types of subsidiary roles. Different subsidiary roles result in different parent-subsidiary relationships (strategic control trajectory, dependence, independence, shared value performance, and strategic focus), and different subsidiary governance structures should be set up to match these varying relationships. The compatibility of the governance structures and strategic roles determines the strategic performance of MNEs (Kim et al., 2005). In an empirical study, Costello and Costello (2010) identified three types of subsidiary governance bundles, categorised based on their dependence on parent-centred governance mechanisms, subsidiary-centred governance mechanisms, or parent- and subsidiary-centred governance mechanisms. They argued that the international strategy of an MNE and the importance, environmental uncertainty, and age of its subsidiary are factors that help predict what type of subsidiary governance bundle the MNE uses to align the interests of its headquarters with those of a particular subsidiary.

Other scholars have examined the parent company's control of subsidiaries through the lenses of agency theory, the knowledge-based view, and social interaction theory. For example, Dimitratos et al. (2010) investigated corporate governance and the extent of the centralisation of decision-making processes in subsidiaries. They distinguished between results-based and behaviour-based incentive/supervisory mechanisms used by parent companies in subsidiary management and conducted an in-depth case study of 14 Greece-based group companies with overseas operations. Globalisation also affects the parent company's governance.

At the parent company level, governance focuses on the division and supervision of the parent company's rights, powers, and duties. Integrating agency theory and social interaction theory, O'Donnell (2000) argued that although agency theory serves as the basis for a model that predicts the use of monitoring mechanisms and incentive compensation, it is insufficient for explaining the subsidiary management mechanisms of MNEs. According to his empirical findings based on data from US-based MNEs, although agency theory could account well for the control issues within MNEs, it fell short in explaining the phenomenon of foreign subsidiary control. For this purpose, models based on intra-firm interdependence had greater explanatory power.

4.2.2 Parent Company Control and Subsidiary Ownership Governance

Connelly et al. (2010) pointed out that firm ownership is an increasingly influential form of corporate governance. In an empirical study of US-based MNEs operating in Mexico, Martinez and Ricks (1989) found that the type of ownership arrangement affected the degree of influence that parent companies had over the human resource decisions of their subsidiaries. However, a high ownership percentage does not necessarily mean a high degree of parental influence. For example, US parent companies may exert significant influence over the human resource decisions of subsidiaries in which they have only a small stake. This influence stems, for example, from the Mexican subsidiaries having higher resource dependence (such as technology dependence) on the US parent company than on the host country parent company. Chang and Taylor (1999) investigated factors determining the degree and type of control used by American and Japanese MNEs on their Korean subsidiaries. They found that the amount of control that the parent company exerted over the output and employees in its foreign subsidiaries (cultural control) increased with the degree of its ownership. The subsidiary size moderated the relationship between the degree of ownership and the amount of employee control. Nell and Ambos (2013) examined parenting advantage in the MNE. They found that the external embeddedness of the MNE was an antecedent to headquarters' value creation and that a parent company's investments in their relationships with the subsidiaries' contexts were positively related to the value-added by the parent company. Furthermore, this relationship was stronger when the subsidiary itself was strongly embedded.

Among the early researchers who introduced ownership into the studies of multinational corporate governance was Schaan (1983), who proposed that MNE parents can influence and control their foreign subsidiaries through the use of several control mechanisms, including such formal documents as technical and management contracts with the board of directors. Schaan found that both US and Japanese MNEs used output control as a major means to control their subsidiaries, but Japanese MNEs exerted a higher degree of cultural control over their subsidiaries in South Korea than US MNEs. Specifically, compared with US MNEs, Japanese MNEs used more output and Japanese top management control (a high degree of cultural control) for their subsidiaries. The study also found that agency costs may be relatively low in Japan, a collectivist society, mainly because Japanese MNEs exert a higher degree of control over subsidiaries.

Much of the literature on MNEs' control over their foreign subsidiaries is based on companies from developed economies. Chang et al. (2009) investigated how parent companies of MNEs in Taiwan controlled their overseas subsidiaries in the UK. They found that MNE parent companies in Taiwan primarily exerted output and behavioural control over their UK subsidiaries. They required these subsidiaries to submit operating cost and productivity data regularly to control their outputs. They exerted behavioural control to ensure that the behaviour, processes, and decisions of UK subsidiaries were consistent with the overall goals of the parent companies. Integrating agency theory with institutional analysis, Liang et al. (2015) proposed a state-control perspective to analyse the government control mechanisms of SOEs in emerging economies. They identified two types of state control affecting SOEs' globalisation decisions: state ownership control and executives' political connections. Based on data on Chinese listed companies, they found a strong impact of both types of state control on SOEs' globalisation.

4.3 MNEs External Network Governance

As an MNE is a type of network organisation, MNE governance has the characteristics of network governance. The internal network governance of an MNE consists of parent company governance and foreign subsidiary governance. The external networks of an MNE refer to the networks composed of host governments, international non-profit organisations (such as environmental protection organisations), suppliers, partners, customers, and other stakeholders, in which its foreign subsidiaries are embedded. Therefore, compared with domestic corporate governance, the MNE's external network governance involves a more complex range of stakeholders, including host governments, partners, and non-profit organisations, relationships with which must be dealt with by foreign subsidiaries.

MNE's external governance has a larger scope than the external governance of domestic companies. The cross-border activities of MNEs greatly expand the group of their stakeholders and expose them to compete in the global product market, factor market, and corporate control market (Li, 2009). MNEs' foreign investments are affected by host country stakeholders, such as host governments and related interest groups. In addition, their foreign subsidiaries, being embedded in both host and home country institutional environments, are subject to the influence of institutional and cultural factors in the home and host countries (Meyer et al., 2011).

Kwok and Tadesse (2006) proposed a theoretical framework for the interaction between host institutions and MNEs. The behaviour of MNEs' foreign subsidiaries is affected by local governments and business groups in the host country (see Fig. 4.1). In turn, the MNE influences the host governments and local business groups and shapes the institutional environment in the host country through regulatory pressure, demonstration, and professionalisation effects. The home country's institutional environment and the activities of other foreign multinational

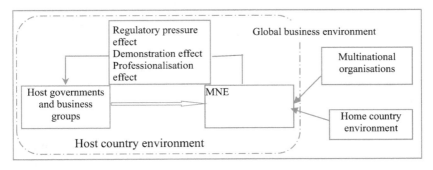

Fig. 4.1 Interaction between MNEs and host country environment

organisations also affect the survival of foreign subsidiaries in the host country.

When engaging in FDI, MNEs are under regulatory pressure from the home country government and multinational business groups (Rodriguez et al., 2005). For example, in the wake of a series of bribery scandals involving US companies in foreign markets, the United States enacted the *Foreign Corrupt Practices Act* in 1977, which prohibits US companies and individuals from paying bribes to foreign officials and requires companies with securities listed in the US to meet specific accounting provisions. Following the lead of the US, other countries, such as Canada, promulgated similar domestic laws, which have now been applied worldwide. On 21 November 1997, representatives from 33 countries signed the Organisation for Economic Cooperation and Development (OECD) Convention on Combating Bribery of Foreign Public Officials in International Business Transactions.

MNEs often encounter government corruption when they operate in host countries. Most of the empirical research in this area has examined how an institutional environment of corruption shapes the behaviour of MNEs. Using an institutional perspective, Rodriguez et al. (2005) examined how the pervasiveness and arbitrariness of corruption can affect an MNE's organisational legitimacy and strategic decision-making. They used a framework that considers pervasiveness and arbitrariness to describe local corruption, which helps MNEs comprehend the challenges of corruption in a particular state and distinguish them from those in other states so as to avert or exploit them. They suggested that firms adapt their entry modes in response to the pervasiveness and arbitrariness of corruption. Cuervo-Cazurra (2006) examined the impact of corruption on FDI. Given that corruption results in relatively lower FDI from countries that have signed the Convention on Combating Bribery of Foreign Public Officials in International Business Transactions and relatively higher FDI from countries with high levels of corruption, he argued that corruption results not only in a reduction in FDI but also in a change in the composition of the country of origin of FDI. Keig et al. (2015) divided corruption environments into two basic types: formal and informal. Using an institutional theory framework, they examined the relationship between corruption environments and MNE social irresponsibility. The results show that higher levels of formal and informal corruption environments found in an MNE's operating portfolio were related to higher levels of corporate social irresponsibility (CSiR).

North (1990) defined institutions as the human-devised constraints that structure human interaction. According to Scott (1995), institutions are composed of cultural-cognitive, normative, and regulative elements that, together with associated activities and resources, provide stability and meaning to social life. Many theorists hold that institutions consist of both formal rules (such as constitutions and laws) and informal constraints (such as codes of conduct) that constitute the rules of the game and the structure of the political, economic, and social interactions in a society or country. On this basis, MNEs inevitably be affected by both host and home country institutions. Chan et al. (2008) investigated the effect of host countries' level of institutional development on the level of, and variations in, foreign affiliate performance. The results indicated that the level of institutional development, as determined by the Institutional Development Index (IDI), had a strong negative curvilinear relationship with the variation in foreign affiliate performance and a negative effect on the level of foreign affiliate performance.

Integrating the institution-based view of strategy with resource-based considerations, Meyer et al. (2009) investigated the impact of market-supporting institutions on business strategies by analysing the entry strategies of foreign investors entering emerging economies. The results suggest that alternative modes of entry, including greenfield, acquisition, and joint venture, allow firms to overcome different kinds of market inefficiencies related to the resources' characteristics and the institutional context. In a weaker institutional framework, joint ventures are used to access many resources, but in a stronger institutional framework, they become less important, and acquisitions can play a more important role in accessing intangible and organisationally embedded resources. Zhang et al. (2011) studied how institutional factors influence the likelihood that Chinese overseas acquisition deals are completed, arguing that the success of a Chinese firm in a cross-border acquisition is an outcome of institutional contingencies at multiple levels. The study found that the likelihood of a Chinese firm to succeed in an overseas acquisition was lower if (1) the target country had poorer institutional quality, (2) the target industry was sensitive to national security, and (3) the acquiring firm was an SOE. In addition, the study found that host country institutions moderated the effect of the two firm-level factors of learning experience and state ownership.

4.3.1 Host Country Institutional and Cultural Influences on Foreign Subsidiary Governance

MNEs are greatly affected by host country institutions. Scholars usually use the concept of institutional distance to measure the institutional differences between home and host countries. The institutional distance was first used in studies of international business and strategy during the 1990s. As the number of studies applying the institution-based view in international business and strategy has surged in the early twenty-fir century, fruitful results have been achieved regarding institutional distance.

In a study of institutional distance and multinational enterprises, Xu and Shenkar (2002) decomposed the institutional distance between the host and home countries into distances on the regulative, normative, and cognitive dimensions of institutions and matched these with firm-level attributes to derive propositions regarding host country selection and foreign market entry strategies. They proposed that institutional distance complements the cultural distance construct and expands the perspective of strategic countermeasures in MNE theories, laying the theoretical foundation for institutional distance and entry mode studies.

Among the empirical studies, Brouthers (2002) proposed an extended transaction cost model including cultural and institutional context variables and examined the institutional, cultural, and transaction cost influences on the foreign market entry mode choice of MNEs. The results show that MNEs were more likely to use the joint venture entry mode in the presence of more legal constraints and higher investment risks. In a study of how regulatory and normative institutional distance affects the ownership choices of MNEs, Eden and Miller (2004) pointed out that MNEs tend to go to extremes by choosing franchising or wholly owned subsidiary models in countries with high regulatory institutional distance, while choosing a moderate strategy (i.e., holding non-controlling shares in subsidiaries) in countries with high normative institutional distance.

In a recent study on the entry modes of foreign investment, Ando (2012) investigated how the institutional distance between home and host countries affects the ownership structure of foreign subsidiaries based on a sample of foreign subsidiaries of Japanese firms. The results indicate that Japanese firms reduced equity shares in foreign subsidiaries as institutional distance increased. This suggests that the institutional distance between home and host countries affects the FDI entry mode choice of MNEs.

Host country cultural influences on MNEs have also drawn considerable attention in recent years. Scholars usually use cultural distance to measure the cultural difference between home and host countries. Unlike psychic distance, cultural distance does not highlight the cognitive differences between individuals (Hofstede, 1980).

Cultural distance increases the 'liability of foreignness'[1] and the difficulty of running a business in foreign countries. The greater the cultural distance of a host country, the more a company has to pay to understand the market and consumer behaviour. In addition, cultural distance makes it more difficult for a company to understand and communicate with its partners, limiting its ability to predict partners' speculative behaviour and resulting in higher investment risks. To reduce the risks from partners' speculative behaviour, the company must spend considerable time and energy monitoring its partners, which increases operation and management costs.

4.3.2 Influence of Host Country Stakeholders on MNEs

The influence of host country stakeholders on MNEs is mainly associated with legitimacy. Legitimacy is 'a generalised perception or assumption that the actions of an entity are desirable, proper, appropriate within some socially constructed system of norms, values, beliefs, and definitions' (Suchman, 1995). Legitimacy is an important resource for the survival and growth of new ventures (Zimmerman & Zeitz, 2002). By gaining and enhancing their legitimacy, new ventures are more likely to survive and achieve long-term development (Meyer & Rowan, 1977). Studies of organisational legitimacy, especially MNE legitimacy, are mostly based on institutional theory, which emphasises the importance of a company's embeddedness in institutional environments, and particularly the influence of embeddedness in the home and host country institutional environments on the legitimacy of foreign subsidiaries. Child and Marinova (2014) pointed out that institutional maturity varies across countries, which means that some countries have a better institutional environment than others regarding legal and regulatory systems, transparency, adherence to clear rules, and universal applicability to all citizens. As a consequence, institutional gaps take shape and form either a surplus

---

[1] Zaheer (1995: 343) defines 'liability of foreignness' as all the additional costs a firm operating in a market overseas incurs that a local firm would not incur.

or deficit. An institutional surplus occurs when the home country has a better institutional environment (a higher quality score) than the host country and an institutional deficit if it is the other way around. For companies from emerging economies, the type of institutional gap has a relatively large impact on their legitimacy during internationalisation (Lin et al., 2012).

4.4 Multinational Corporate Governance: An Integrated Network Governance Framework

In summary, as network organisations, MNEs are embedded in external networks composed of customers, suppliers, and governments, within which their business units must interact with each other. MNEs have become a major driving force of economic globalisation. To boost their development, corporate governance research must use a broader range of perspectives to explore how to integrate the resources of various stakeholders through effective corporate governance and thereby establish and maintain sustainable competitive advantages. Multinational corporate governance is related to a single company's governance and the network governance of a parent-subsidiary network organisation. A central issue in a network organisation is how to distribute the decision-making power reasonably. The governance of an MNE is expanded to include dynamic interactions between the home country, host countries, and the MNE, which gives it different characteristics from those of domestic corporate governance.

Corporate governance of an MNE mainly includes governance at four levels: parent company governance, subsidiary governance, parent-subsidiary relationship governance, and external governance. External governance is of particular interest because of the changes in the governance environment, such as institutional and cultural changes that take place during internationalisation. The framework for MNE network governance is shown in Fig. 4.2.

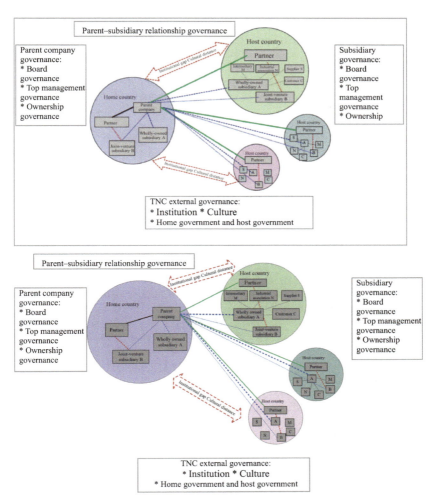

Fig. 4.2 MNE network governance framework

References

Alpay, G., Bodur, M., Ener, H., & Talug, C. (2005). Comparing board-level governance at MNEs and local firms: Lessons from Turkey. *Journal of International Management, 11*(1), 67–86.

Anderson, E., & Gatignon, H. (1986). Modes of foreign entry: A transaction cost analysis and propositions. *Journal of International Business Studies, 17*, 1–26.

Andersson, U., & Forsgren, M. (1996). Subsidiary embeddedness and control in the multinational corporation. *International Business Review, 5*(5), 487–508.

Ando, N. (2012). The ownership structure of foreign subsidiaries and the effect of institutional distance: A case study of Japanese firms. *Asia Pacific Business Review, 18*(2), 259–274.

Birkinshaw, J. M., & Morrison, A. J. (1995). Configurations of strategy and structure in subsidiaries of multinational corporations. *Journal of International Business Studies, 26*, 729–753.

Brouthers, K. D. (2002). Institutional, cultural and transaction cost influences on entry mode choice and performance [J]. *Journal of International Business Studies, 33*(2), 203–221.

Brouthers, K. D., & Hennart, J. F. (2007). Boundaries of the firm: Insights from international entry mode research. *Journal of Management, 33*(3), 395–425.

Cantwell, J. (2009). Location and the multinational enterprise. *Journal of International Business Studies, 40*(1), 35–41.

Carpenter, M. A., & Sanders, W. G. (2004). The effects of top management team pay and firm internationalisation on MNC performance [J]. *Journal of Management, 30*(4), 509–528.

Chan, C. M., Isobe, T., & Makino, S. (2008). Which country matters? Institutional development and foreign affiliate performance. *Strategic Management Journal, 29*(11), 1179–1205.

Chan, C. M., & Makino, S. (2007). Legitimacy and multi-level institutional environments: Implications for foreign subsidiary ownership structure. *Journal of International Business Studies, 38*(4), 621–638.

Chang, E., & Taylor, M. S. (1999). Control in multinational corporations (MNCs): The case of Korean manufacturing subsidiaries [J]. *Journal of Management, 25*(4), 541–565.

Chang, Y. Y., Mellahi, K., & Wilkinson, A. (2009). Control of subsidiaries of MNCs from emerging economies in developed countries: The case of Taiwanese MNCs in the UK. *International Journal of Human Resource Management, 20*(1), 75–95.

Chen, G., Firth, M., & Xu, L. (2009). Does the type of ownership control matter? Evidence from China's listed companies. *Journal of Banking & Finance, 33*(1), 171–181.

Chen, H. L. (2011). Does board independence influence the top management team? Evidence from strategic decisions toward internationalisation. *Corporate Governance: An International Review, 19*(4), 334–350.

Child, J., & Marinova, S. (2014). Reflections on the commentaries. *Management and Organisation Review, 10*(3), 405–409.

Cho, K. R., Huang, C. H., & Padmanabhan, P. (2014). Foreign ownership mode, executive compensation structure, and corporate governance: Has the literature missed an important link? Evidence from Taiwanese firms. *International Business Review, 23*(2), 371–380.

Clark, C., & Brown, J. A. (2014). Multinational corporations and governance reform: Towards a more integrative board. *Academy of Management Proceedings. Academy of Management, 2014*(1), 12880.

Connelly, B. L., Hoskisson, R. E., Tihanyi, L., & Certo, S. T. (2010). Ownership as a form of corporate governance. *Journal of Management Studies, 47*(8), 1561–1589.

Costello, A., & Costello, T. (2010). Aligning the interests of subsidiaries and headquarters in multinational corporations. *Multinational Business Review, 17*(4), 163–204.

Cuervo-Cazurra, A. (2006). Who cares about corruption? *Journal of International Business Studies, 37*(6), 807–822.

Cui, L., & Jiang, F. (2012). State ownership effect on Firms' FDI ownership decisions under institutional pressure: A study of Chinese outward-investing firms. *Journal of International Business Studies, 43*(3), 264–284.

Demirbag, M., Tatoglu, E., & Glaister, K. W. (2009). Equity-based entry modes of emerging country multinationals: Lessons from Turkey. *Journal of World Business, 44*(4), 445–462.

Denis, D. K., & McConnell, J. J. (2003). International corporate governance. *Journal of Financial and Quantitative Analysis, 38*(01), 1–36.

Dimitratos, P., Lioukas, S., Ibeh, K. I. N., et al. (2010). Governance mechanisms of small and medium enterprise international partner management. *British Journal of Management, 21*(3), 754–771.

Donaldson, L., & Davis, J. H. (1994). Boards and company performance—Research challenges the conventional wisdom. *Corporate Governance: An International Review, 2*(3), 151–160.

Du, Y., Deloof, M., & Jorissen, A. (2011). Active boards of directors in foreign subsidiaries. *Corporate Governance: An International Review, 19*(2), 153–168.

Du, Y., Deloof, M., & Jorissen, A. (2015). The roles of subsidiary boards in multinational enterprises. *Journal of International Management, 21*(3), 169–181.

Eden, L., & Miller, S. R. (2004). Distance matters: Liability of foreignness, institutional distance and ownership strategy. *Advances in International Management, 16*, 187–221.

Erramilli, M. K., & Rao, C. P. (1993). Service firms' international entry-mode choice: A modified transaction-cost analysis approach. *The Journal of Marketing, 57*(3), 19–38.

Fey, C. F., & Furu, P. (2008). Top management incentive compensation and knowledge sharing in multinational corporations. *Strategic Management Journal, 29*(12), 1301–1323.

Filatotchev, I., Dyomina, N., Wright, M., & Buck, T. (2001). Effects of post-privatisation governance and strategies on export intensity in the former Soviet Union. *Journal of International Business Studies, 32,* 853–871.

Filatotchev, I., Stephan, J., & Jindra, B. (2008). Ownership structure, strategic controls and export intensity of foreign-invested firms in transition economies. *Journal of International Business Studies, 39*(7), 1133–1148.

Finkelstein, S., & Hambrick, D. C. (1996). *Strategic leadership: Top executives and their effects on organisations.* South-Western Pub.

Gaur, A. S., & Lu, J. W. (2007). Ownership strategies and survival of foreign subsidiaries: Impacts of institutional distance and experience. *Journal of Management, 33*(1), 84–110.

Ghoshal, S., & Bartlett, C. A. (1990). The multinational corporation as an interorganisational network. *Academy of Management Review, 15*(4), 603–626.

Gomes-Casseres, B. (1989). Ownership structures of foreign subsidiaries: Theory and evidence. *Journal of Economic Behaviour & Organisation, 11*(1), 1–25.

Gomes-Casseres, B. (1990). Firm ownership preferences and host government restrictions: An integrated approach. *Journal of International Business Studies, 21*(1), 1–22.

Gong, Y. (2006). The impact of subsidiary top management team national diversity on subsidiary performance: Knowledge and legitimacy perspectives. *Management International Review, 46*(6), 771–790.

Gupta, A. K., & Govindarajan, V. (2000). Knowledge flows within multinational corporations. *Strategic Management Journal, 21*(4), 473–496.

Hambrick, D. C., & Mason, P. A. (1984). Upper echelons: The organisation as a reflection of its top managers. *Academy of Management Review, 9*(2), 193–206.

Herrmann, P., & Datta, D. K. (2005). Relationships between top management team Characteristics and international diversification: An empirical investigation. *British Journal of Management, 16*(1), 69–78.

Hill, C. W. L., Hwang, P., & Kim, W. C. (1990). An eclectic theory of the choice of international entry mode. *Strategic Management Journal, 11*(2), 117–128.

Hofstede, G. (1980). *Cultural consequences.* Sage.

Jensen, M. C., & Meckling, W. H. (1976). Theory of the firm: Managerial behaviour, agency costs and ownership structure. *Journal of Financial Economics, 3*(4), 305–360.

Keig, D. L., Brouthers, L. E., & Marshall, V. B. (2015). Formal and informal corruption environments and multinational enterprise social irresponsibility. *Journal of Management Studies, 52*(1), 89–116.

Kiel, G. C., Hendry, K., & Nicholson, G. J. (2006). Corporate governance options for the local subsidiaries of multinational enterprises. *Corporate Governance: An International Review, 14*(6), 568–576.

Kilduff, M., & Tsai, W. (2003). *Social networks and organisations*. Sage.

Kim, B., Prescott, J. E., & Kim, S. M. (2005). Differentiated governance of foreign subsidiaries in multinational corporations: An agency theory perspective. *Journal of International Management, 11*(1), 43–66.

Kor, Y. Y. (2006). Direct and interaction effects of top management team and board compositions on R&D investment strategy. *Strategic Management Journal, 27*(11), 1081–1099.

Kostova, T., & Roth, K. (2002). Adoption of an organisational practice by subsidiaries of multinational corporations: Institutional and relational effects. *Academy of Management Journal, 45*(1), 215–233.

Kostova, T., Roth, K., & Dacin, M. T. (2008). Institutional theory in the study of multinational corporations: A critique and new directions. *Academy of Management Review, 33*(4), 994–1006.

Kostova, T., & Zaheer, S. (1999). Organisational legitimacy under conditions of complexity: The case of the multinational enterprise. *Academy of Management Review, 24*(1), 64–81.

Kriger, M. P. (1988). The increasing role of subsidiary boards in MNCs: An empirical study. *Strategic Management Journal, 9*(4), 347–360.

Kwok, C. C. Y., & Tadesse, S. (2006). The MNC as an agent of change for host-country institutions: FDI and corruption. *Journal of International Business Studies, 37*(6), 767–785.

Leksell, L., & Lindgren, U. (1982). The board of directors in foreign subsidiaries. *Journal of International Business Studies, 13*, 27–38.

Li, W. A. (2009). *Corporate governance* (2nd ed.). Higher Education Press.

Li, et al. (2011). Recent developments in corporate governance research: International trends and Chinese model. *Nankai Business Review, 2011*(6), 13–24.

Liang, H., Ren, B., & Sun, S. L. (2015). An anatomy of state control in the globalisation of state-owned enterprises. *Journal of International Business Studies, 46*(2), 223–240.

Lien, Y. C., Piesse, J., Strange, R., et al. (2005). The role of corporate governance in FDI decisions: Evidence from Taiwan. *International Business Review, 14*(6), 739–763.

Lin, R. H., Xu, Ye. K., Fan, J. H, Zhang, H. J., & Fei, W. Y. (2012). Entry mode choices of multinational corporations—A framework for theoretical analysis. *Corporate Governance Review, 2012*(2).

Lu, J., Liu, X., Filatotchev, I., & Wright, M. (2014). The impact of domestic diversification and top management teams on the international diversification of Chinese firms. *International Business Review, 23*(2), 455–467.

Lu, J., Xu, B., & Liu, X. (2009). The effects of corporate governance and institutional environments on export behaviour in emerging economies. *Management International Review, 49*(4), 455–478.

Luo, Y. D. (2005). Corporate governance and accountability in multinational enterprises: Concepts and agenda. *Journal of International Management, 11*(1), 1–18.

Luo, Y., & Tung, R. L. (2007). International expansion of emerging market enterprises: A springboard perspective. *Journal of International Business Studies, 38*(4), 481–498.

Martinez, Z. L., & Ricks, D. A. (1989). Multinational parent companies' Influence over human resource decisions of affiliates: US firms in Mexico. *Journal of International Business Studies, 20*, 465–487.

McDonald, M. L., Khanna, P., & Westphal, J. D. (2008). Getting them to think outside the circle: Corporate governance, CEOs' external advice networks, and firm performance. *Academy of Management Journal, 51*(3), 453–475.

Meyer, K. E., Estrin, S., Bhaumik, S., & Peng, M. W. (2009). Institutions, resources, and entry strategies in emerging economies. *Strategic Management Journal, 30*(1), 61–80.

Meyer, M., Milgrom, P., & Roberts, J. (1992). Organisational prospects, influence costs, and ownership changes. *Journal of Economics & Management Strategy, 1*(1), 9–35.

Meyer, K. E., Mudambi, R., & Narula, R. (2011). Multinational enterprises and local contexts: The opportunities and challenges of multiple embeddedness. *Journal of Management Studies, 48*(2), 235–252.

Meyer, J. W., & Rowan, B. (1977). Institutionalized organizations: Formal structure as myth and ceremony. *American Journal of Sociology, 83*, 340–363.

Monteiro, L. F., Arvidsson, N., & Birkinshaw, J. (2008). Knowledge flows within multinational corporations: Explaining subsidiary isolation and its performance implications. *Organisation Science, 19*(1), 90–107.

Musteen, M., Datta, D. K., & Herrmann, P. (2009). Ownership structure and CEO compensation: Implications for the choice of foreign market entry modes. *Journal of International Business Studies, 40*(2), 321–338.

Nell, P. C., & Ambos, B. (2013). Parenting advantage in the MNC: An embeddedness perspective on the value added by headquarters. *Strategic Management Journal, 34*(9), 1086–1103.

Nielsen, B. B., & Nielsen, S. (2013). Top management team nationality diversity and firm performance: A multilevel study. *Strategic Management Journal, 34*(3), 373–382.

Nohria, N., & Ghoshal, S. (1997). *The differentiated network: Organising multinational corporations for value creation*. Jossey-Bass Publishers.

North, D. C. (1990). *Institutions*. Cambridge University Press.

O'Donnell, S. W. (2000). Managing foreign subsidiaries: Agents of headquarters, or an interdependent network? *Strategic Management Journal, 21*(5), 525–548.

Piekkari, R., Oxelheim, L., & Randøy, T. (2015). The silent board: How language diversity may influence the work processes of corporate boards. *Corporate Governance: An International Review, 23*(1), 25–41.

Reuer, J. J., Klijn, E., & Lioukas, C. S. (2014). Board involvement in international joint ventures. *Strategic Management Journal, 35*(11), 1626–1644.

Rivas, J. L. (2012). Diversity & internationalisation: The case of boards and TMTs. *International Business Review, 21*(1), 1–12.

Rodriguez, P., Uhlenbruck, K., & Eden, L. (2005). Government corruption and the entry strategies of multinationals. *Academy of Management Review, 30*(2), 383–396.

Roth, K., & Morrison, A. J. (1992). Implementing global strategy: Characteristics of global subsidiary mandates. *Journal of International Business Studies, 23*, 715–735.

Roth, K., & O'Donnell, S. (1996). Foreign subsidiary compensation strategy: An agency theory perspective. *Academy of Management Journal, 39*(3), 678–703.

Sambharya, R. B. (1996). Research notes and communications: Foreign experience of top management teams and international diversification strategies of US multinational corporations. *Strategic Management Journal, 1996*(17), 739–746.

Sanders, W. M. G., & Carpenter, M. A. (1998). Internationalisation and firm governance: The roles of CEO compensation, top team composition, and board structure. *Academy of Management Journal, 41*(2), 158–178.

Schaan, J. L. (1983). *Parent control and joint venture success: The case of Mexico.* Unpublished PhD Thesis, University of Western Ontario, Canada.

Scott, W. R. (1995). *Institutions and organisations.* Sage.

Sekiguchi, T., Bebenroth, R., & Li, D. (2011). Nationality background of MNC affiliates' top management and affiliate performance in Japan: Knowledge-based and upper echelons perspectives. *The International Journal of Human Resource Management, 22*(05), 999–1016.

Suchman, M. C. (1995). Managing legitimacy: Strategic and institutional approaches. *Academy of Management Review, 20*(3), 574.

Xie, Q. (2014). CEO tenure and ownership mode choice of Chinese firms: The moderating roles of managerial discretion. *International Business Review, 23*(5), 910–919.

Xu, D., & Shenkar, O. (2002). Note: Institutional distance and the multinational enterprise. *Academy of Management Review, 27*(4), 608–618.

Zaheer, S. (1995). Overcoming the liability of foreignness [J]. *Academy of Management Journal, 38*(2), 341–363.

Zaheer, A., Gulati, R., & Nohria, N. (2000). Strategic networks. *Strategic Management Journal*, *21*(3), 203.

Zhang, J., Zhou, C., & Ebbers, H. (2011). Completion of Chinese overseas acquisitions: Institutional perspectives and evidence. *International Business Review*, *20*(2), 226–238.

Zhou, J., Yin, C. F., & Chen, S. R. (2013). A study on the influence of board attributes on corporate internationalisation strategy. *Management Review*, *25*(011), 133–143.

Zhou, J., Yu, W., & Liu, X. Y. (2008). A review and outlook for studies of multinational corporate governance. *Foreign Economics and Management*, *2008*, 1–8.

Zimmerman, M. A., & Zeitz, G. J. (2002). Beyond survival: Achieving new venture growth by building legitimacy. *Academy of Management Review*, *27*(3), 414–431.

CHAPTER 5

Foreign Subsidiary Governance

As the implementers of MNEs' global strategies, foreign subsidiaries are of strategic importance to the parent company. Foreign subsidiary governance is a key issue in research into multinational corporate governance. Foreign subsidiaries are embedded in networks composed of host governments, international non-profit organisations (such as environmental protection organisations and local labour unions), partners, customers, and other stakeholders. As a result of this complex range of stakeholders, their governance is much more complicated than domestic corporate governance. Therefore, foreign subsidiary governance merits a separate discussion to which this chapter is devoted.

Multinational corporate governance is, in essence, a type of network governance (Lin et al., 2009). It differs from group governance in the ordinary sense because foreign subsidiaries play different strategic roles in a multinational context. Subsidiaries are embedded in a network of customers, suppliers, and governments in host countries. They are also affected by the parent company, other foreign subsidiaries, and the home government. The relationships between foreign subsidiaries and local organisations (such as customers, suppliers, and government agencies) in host countries form their external networks (Andersson et al., 2002; Ghoshal & Bartlett, 1990). Therefore, the governance of foreign subsidiaries is related to both single company governance and network governance. How to reasonably distribute the decision-making power in

© The Author(s), under exclusive license to Springer Nature Singapore Pte Ltd. 2022
R. Lin and J. J. Chen, *The Theory and Application of Multinational Corporate Governance*, https://doi.org/10.1007/978-981-16-7703-8_5

such networks remains the central concern. The governance of foreign subsidiaries is expanded to include dynamic interactions between the host countries, MNEs, and the home country, showing different characteristics from the governance of domestic companies.

Taking a network governance perspective, this chapter first discusses the internal governance of foreign subsidiaries as key nodes of a network organisation, then analyses the governance of parent-subsidiary relationships, and finally explores the external governance of foreign subsidiaries.

5.1 Internal Governance of Foreign Subsidiaries of MNEs

Each foreign subsidiary of an MNE undertakes unique tasks and roles in its host country and its specific role restricts or determines its operations (Rosenzweig & Singh, 1991). The governance structure and mechanism of a foreign subsidiary play an important role in MNEs' responses to the uncertainty and complexity of the host country's environment (Kriger, 1988). This chapter discusses aspects of the internal governance of foreign subsidiaries of MNEs, focusing on board governance, equity governance, senior management governance, and parent-subsidiary relationship governance.

5.1.1 Board Governance

In foreign subsidiaries, the board of directors serves as an important internal governance mechanism and a connecting mechanism for obtaining local resources, and its roles can be summarised as control, strategy, coordination, and service (Du et al., 2015). Control means that it supervises and approves important decisions of foreign subsidiaries and evaluates the performance and management thereof (Kriger, 1988). Strategy means that it plays the same role as the board of a completely independent company by participating in the strategic planning, identifying the strategic direction, and evaluating the strategic plans of foreign subsidiaries. Coordination refers to the board's task of transferring information and knowledge between the headquarters of an MNE and its foreign subsidiaries. Service mainly includes providing localisation knowledge to the management of foreign subsidiaries and communicating with local stakeholders to ensure that subsidiaries have easier access to local resources. The literature on the subsidiary board is mainly based on agency theory, resource dependence theory, resource-based theory, and upper echelons theory.

5.1.1.1 From the Perspective of Agency Theory
Scholars adopting an agency theory perspective study the role of the subsidiary board in MNEs' control over their foreign operations. However, their research mainly focuses on how parent companies control foreign subsidiaries through the subsidiary board without considering the self-governance of foreign subsidiaries.

Early studies tended to focus on the supervisory role of the subsidiary board, which can reduce environmental uncertainty in the host country and respond flexibly to external changes. The role of the subsidiary board of an MNE is different from that of a single company. When the goals pursued by managers of foreign subsidiaries of MNEs conflict with those of parent companies, agency problems arise. By supervising the performance of managers of foreign subsidiaries, the subsidiary board ensures that the strategic decisions made by management conform to the overall goals of the parent companies, thus reducing these agency problems (Jensen & Meckling, 1976).

In addition, the subsidiary board not only acts as a supervisory mechanism but also as a strategic governance mechanism. Foreign subsidiaries of MNEs can be assigned any of three strategic roles: local implementer, specialised contributor, and world mandate. From the perspective of agency, compared with foreign subsidiaries operating as world mandates or specialised contributors, local implementers are more likely to have agency problems because they operate independently of other subsidiaries of their parents. When such subsidiaries get information about local markets, they usually do not provide it to the headquarters. Furthermore, to ensure a rapid response to local market demand, local implementers can make strategic and operational decisions on their own (Birkinshaw & Morrison, 1995), which makes them more difficult for the parent company to supervise and control (Kiel et al., 2006). Du et al. (2015) found that foreign subsidiaries operating as world mandates were more closely related to their parent companies and showed a higher level of local responsiveness.

5.1.1.2 From the Perspective of Resource Dependence Theory

Resource dependence theory states that as a resource provider, the board of directors can provide advice and counsel, legitimacy, channels of communication with external organisations, and access to external resources and support. The subsidiary board maintains ties with the stakeholders in the host country to seek access to important knowledge and resources for MNEs. The competitive edge of MNEs usually comes from the unique knowledge of their foreign subsidiaries (Gupta & Govindarajan, 2000; Monteiro et al., 2008). Foreign subsidiaries are engaged in a network of relationships with local stakeholders (such as customers, suppliers, and management agencies) to obtain important resources (Cantwell, 2009), thus reducing dependence on local resources.

5.1.1.3 From the Resource-Based Perspective

Unlike resource dependence theory, the resource-based view holds that the expertise, experience and skills of the board of directors and senior executives of foreign subsidiaries are valuable and inimitable resources of the organisation, which can reduce its dependence on the external environment, external uncertainty, and transaction costs. These resources are necessary for the organisation to build and maintain a sustainable competitive edge.

The composition of the subsidiary board is critical. Inside directors have the specialised knowledge for making business decisions, but they cannot objectively evaluate the strategic decision-making process under the CEO's influence. Outside directors, meanwhile, lack enterprise-specific knowledge and cannot understand the complexity of the company's business. Donaldson and Davis (1994) found that foreign subsidiaries with a high proportion of inside directors could make decisions more quickly, leading to higher performance. Therefore, a reasonable composition of the subsidiary board constitutes an important resource base for foreign subsidiaries of MNEs.

5.1.2 Equity Governance

How MNEs control and manage foreign subsidiaries internally and address the liability of foreignness faced by new foreign subsidiaries externally, have become the focus of attention of scholars in China and abroad. Equity-based control was an important topic in early studies of MNE governance (Demirbag et al., 2009; Luo & Tung, 2007; Woodcock et al., 1994). Equity, equivalent to the resource commitment of a parent company to its foreign subsidiaries (Chan & Makino, 2007), is the result of negotiation between MNEs and host governments or local authorities, reflecting the relative bargaining power of both parties. Equity implies a parent company's right to control the operation and strategic decisions of its foreign subsidiaries.

Research on the equity of foreign subsidiaries of MNEs has seen an evolution of theoretical perspective from early transaction cost theory to institutional theory and upper echelons theory, and a change of research object from the equity governance of foreign subsidiaries in developed economies to that in emerging economies.

5.1.2.1 *From the Perspective of Transaction Cost Theory*

Anderson and Gatignon (1986) early study took the perspective of transaction cost theory to posit that the most efficient entry mode was a function of a trade-off between control and resource input costs. Their study found that a higher degree of ownership was associated with more invested resources, higher input costs, and a higher degree of control. Moreover, with an increase in transaction costs, MNEs may tend to own all of the shares of their subsidiaries to reduce transaction risks (Erramilli & Rao, 1993). Thus, some scholars believe that the traditional theories should be discarded for the study of MNEs and replaced with a theoretical model that binds MNEs with local resources from the perspective of the evolution of MNEs. Such a new model would be able to predict the evolution of MNEs in host countries by examining, for example, whether the equity is held by MNEs or local companies or shared by both, and whether an MNE chooses to enter the local market through a new venture, joint venture, or acquisition.

In summary, for studying the equity governance of foreign subsidiaries, transaction cost theory only considers the entry efficiency and costs, thus neglecting the potential impacts of external environmental factors.

5.1.2.2 *From the Perspective of Institutional Theory*

Unlike the efficiency-oriented transaction cost theory, the institutional theory mainly focuses on the legitimacy problems of foreign subsidiaries, which are attributed to the liabilities of foreignness and newness, in explaining the entry mode of MNEs (Kostova & Roth, 2002; Kostova, 1999; Xu & Shenkar, 2002). A foreign subsidiary faces isomorphic pressures from the host country and its parent company and needs legitimacy within both. This institutional duality affects the governance of foreign subsidiaries (Kostova et al., 2008). MNEs favour a lower level of control and resource commitment to build external legitimacy for foreign subsidiaries and often share ownership with local partner companies. Chen et al. (2009) provided evidence for this in the transitional economy of China.

Further research is needed to examine whether the institutional and cultural distances affect the choice and outcomes of MNEs' entry mode and whether the interaction between institutional factors and other decision-making behaviours affects the final decision (Brouthers & Hennart, 2007).

5.1.2.3 From Multi-theoretical Perspective

As no single theoretical perspective is sufficient to explain the equity governance of foreign subsidiaries of MNEs from emerging economies, a multi-theoretical perspective should be adopted. Recent studies have explored the equity governance of foreign subsidiaries of MNEs from emerging economies from the perspectives of political relevance and upper echelons theory. For example, Cui and Jiang (2012), who adopted the perspective of political science to study the equity-related decision-making of Chinese SOEs entering foreign markets, argued that government equity carries the political attributes of home country governments to foreign subsidiaries, which increases foreign subsidiaries' dependence on the resources of home country institutions and affects the image of SOEs in host country governments. Their empirical findings were that control from home countries and host countries and regulation by host countries made SOEs more inclined to choose joint venture as an entry mode, with SOEs having a higher ownership stake in foreign subsidiaries. However, different findings were obtained by Pan et al. (2014), who applied political science and transaction cost theory to their empirical study of foreign subsidiaries of Chinese listed companies and found that enterprises with a higher level of government ownership and those with more political connections held a lower ownership stake in foreign subsidiaries in host countries with an unstable institutional environment. They concluded that these two types of enterprises could eliminate the risks brought by the institutional environment of host countries. Ang et al. (2014) analysed a sample of foreign subsidiaries of MNEs from emerging economies and found evidence of MNEs imitating the ownership model of local companies when making equity-related decisions for foreign subsidiaries. Examining the internal governance of Chinese MNEs, Xie (2014) found that CEO tenure was positively correlated with the number of wholly-owned foreign subsidiaries.

In summary, research into the equity governance of foreign subsidiaries of MNEs often involves two or more theories instead of a single one. The main theories used in this field are transaction cost theory, institutional theory, upper echelons theory, and theories from political science. Most studies have adopted empirical methods, with other research methods, such as case studies, seldom used.

5.1.3 *Senior Management Governance*

Research on senior management governance mainly concerns the influence of the background characteristics of senior management on the strategies of foreign subsidiaries and the influence of the incentive and restraint mechanism and relationship network of senior management on the knowledge flow within MNEs. Most of the literature uses upper echelons theory, incentive mechanism theory, and knowledge-based view to study how the characteristics of, and the incentive mechanisms for, the senior management of foreign subsidiaries affect MNEs' strategies.

1. Upper echelons and knowledge-based theories are used to explain the influence of the characteristics of senior management on the strategies of foreign subsidiaries. The strategic role of foreign subsidiaries and their influencing factors have always been a popular topic for research into the strategic management of MNEs. Early research mainly used upper echelons theory to analyse the relationship between senior management characteristics and foreign subsidiaries' strategies. According to upper echelons theory, the behaviour of foreign subsidiaries reflects the behaviour of senior management (Hambrick & Mason, 1984), and the observable differences in the background characteristics of senior management affect their values, cognition, beliefs, and knowledge base, which together determine their strategic decisions (Finkelstein & Hambrick, 1996; Herrmann & Datta, 2005). The strategic decisions of foreign subsidiaries are usually made through interaction, consultation, and debate among senior executives (Kor, 2006).

Recent studies have combined upper echelons theory with the knowledge-based view and institutional theory to explain the strategic issues involved with foreign subsidiaries. Sekiguchi et al. (2011) undertook a study of 643 foreign subsidiaries from 31 countries operating in Japan based on the knowledge-based view and upper echelons theory. They found that when foreign subsidiaries operated in host countries for long enough, executives of the host country nationality performed better at managing local employees and obtaining legitimacy than executives dispatched by parent companies. However, in the initial stage of operations, executives dispatched by parent companies delivered better performance. Gong (2006) studied the senior management of foreign subsidiaries of Japanese MNEs from the perspectives of knowledge and legitimacy and found that the nationality heterogeneity of senior management was positively correlated with the performance of subsidiaries.

2. Incentive mechanism theory and the knowledge-based view are used to study foreign subsidiaries' performance and knowledge flow. To study the impact of executive compensation and incentive mechanisms of MNEs' foreign subsidiaries on the knowledge flow within MNEs, Fey and Furu (2008) analysed a sample of 164 foreign subsidiaries located in Finland and China in an attempt to identify the relationship between subsidiary bonus pay based on MNE-wide performance and knowledge sharing between different subsidiaries of the MNE. Drawing on a knowledge-based perspective of the firm, they concluded that incentive pay based on the collective performance of the MNE leads to greater knowledge sharing.

5.2 Parent-Subsidiary Relationship Governance

5.2.1 *Parent-Subsidiary Relationship Governance of MNEs in Developed Countries*

5.2.1.1 *Parent-Subsidiary Relationship Governance and the Strategic Role of Foreign Subsidiaries*

Early research into the relationship between parent and subsidiary companies mainly focused on establishing subsidiary mandate frameworks within the scope of MNEs in developed countries (Roth & Morrison, 1992). Under these frameworks, MNEs establish subsidiaries with various strategic mandates that give them access to unique resources or capabilities to fulfil their mandated tasks, and the parent companies' goals play a dominant role in the operation and decision-making of subsidiaries and their strategic agenda in the global production networks of MNEs (Filatotchev et al., 2008). In particular, foreign subsidiaries created through the acquisition of local enterprises can leverage existing dynamic capabilities and knowledge to identify new market opportunities and better complete their tasks.

Kim et al. (2005) constructed a framework for MNEs' governance of foreign subsidiaries drawing on the integration-response analysis framework, pointing out that the differences in parent-subsidiary relationships are mainly affected by host countries, and subsidiaries' institutional environments own capabilities. Meanwhile, different strategic roles of subsidiaries correspond to different parent-subsidiary relationships (strategic control trajectory, dependence, independence, performance of shared value, and strategic focus). Different subsidiary governance structures are needed for different parent-subsidiary relationships, and only when the two are well-matched can MNEs achieve high strategic performance. The empirical study of Costello and Costello (2010) identified three types of subsidiary governance mechanisms: parent-centred, subsidiary-centred, and parent- and subsidiary-centred. The results of their study suggest that MNEs' multinational strategies, the importance of foreign subsidiaries, the environmental uncertainty facing foreign subsidiaries, and the age of foreign subsidiaries can all help predict which governance mechanism MNEs choose.

5.2.1.2 *Parent-Subsidiary Relationship Governance of MNEs Based on Agency Theory, the Knowledge-Based View, and Social Interaction Theory*

Some scholars have studied parent companies' control over subsidiaries from the perspectives of agency theory, the knowledge-based view, and the social interaction theory. For example, Dimitratos et al. (2010) conducted an in-depth case analysis of 14 Greek group companies with foreign operations to study the extent to which the governance and decision-making process is centralised in foreign subsidiaries. They distinguished between two types of incentive and supervision schemes used by parent companies in managing foreign subsidiaries: result-based and behaviour-based. The internationalisation of enterprises also influences parent companies' governance. In a study of American MNEs based on agency theory and social interaction theory, O'Donnell (2000) found that although agency theory could explain the control problem of MNEs, it could not fully account for the phenomenon of foreign subsidiary control or branch control of MNEs, which could be better explained by intercompany interdependence theory. From a knowledge-based perspective, Yan et al. (2004) proposed that with an increase in the actual control of intangible assets, such as knowledge, in foreign subsidiaries, MNEs should intensify the control over their subsidiaries in terms of asset specialisation and interdependence.

5.2.2 Parent-Subsidiary Relationship Governance of MNEs in Emerging Markets

Most studies of how MNEs control their foreign subsidiaries are based on MNEs from developed economies. However, Chang et al. (2009) probed into how the parent companies of MNEs in Taiwan were controlling their foreign subsidiaries based in the UK. Unlike the findings of Chang and Taylor (1999), they found that these parent companies controlled their foreign subsidiaries mainly through output control and behaviour control. The UK-based foreign subsidiaries regularly submitted operating costs and productivity data to their parent companies to facilitate output control. The subsidiaries were also subject to behaviour control to ensure that their behaviours, processes, and decisions were consistent with the overall goals of their parent companies. Integrating agency theory and institutional analysis theory, Liang et al. (2015) analysed the government control mechanism of SOE in emerging economies from the perspective of government control. They identified two types of government control that affect the globalisation-related decision-making of SOEs: state-owned equity control and the political connections of senior managements. Using data on listed companies in China, they found that these two types of control had a substantial impact on the globalisation of SOEs.

5.3 External Governance of Foreign Subsidiaries

The external governance of foreign subsidiaries of MNEs has a broader scope than that of ordinary domestic enterprises. The multinational activities of MNEs greatly expand the range of stakeholders and expose the companies to global product market competition, factor market competition, and corporate control market competition (Li, 2009). The foreign investment of MNEs is affected by host country factors, such as the host government and stakeholders. Foreign subsidiaries of MNEs are embedded in the dual institutional environments of the host country and home country and are directly influenced by the institutions and cultures of both (Meyer et al., 2011). The literature on the survival and development of foreign subsidiaries in a host country has studied the influence of stakeholders, institutions, and culture in the host country discussed how to avoid political risks and the liability of foreignness and provided suggestions on how to acquire legitimacy.

5.3.1 *How Host Country Stakeholders Affect Foreign Subsidiaries*

The operation of foreign subsidiaries is bound to be influenced by host governments and local businesses. How to deal with local players is a top concern of scholars and in business circles. Kwok and Tadesse (2006) put forward a theoretical framework for the interaction between foreign subsidiaries of MNEs, host governments, and local businesses. They posited that foreign subsidiary of MNEs could influence host governments and local businesses over time through the effects of regulatory pressure, demonstration, and professionalisation and further shape the institutional environment in host countries. Meanwhile, the institutional environment in home countries and other multinational business organisations also influence the survival and development of foreign subsidiaries of MNEs.

5.3.2 *How Host Countries' Institutions and Cultures Affect Foreign Subsidiaries*

According to the school of institutional theory, the influence of host countries' institutions and cultures on foreign subsidiaries is mainly felt in the unfamiliarity of a host country's institutional and cultural environment, which is the so-called liability of foreignness. To realise long-term development, foreign subsidiaries need to gain legitimacy (Xu & Shenkar, 2002). Most of the research on organisational legitimacy, especially on the legitimacy of foreign subsidiaries of MNEs, has been based on the institutional theory. This research emphasises the effect of enterprises' embeddedness in the institutional environment, especially the influence of home and host institutional environments on the legitimacy strategies of foreign subsidiaries of MNEs (Meyer et al., 2011). A particular concern is how foreign subsidiaries of MNEs strategically adapt to the constantly changing social and economic environment of emerging economies with transitional institutional environments and gain legitimacy for sustainable operation. In an empirical study of 180 foreign subsidiaries of MNEs operating in China, Zhao et al. (2014) found that improper social adaptation activities on the part of MNEs could lead to a legitimacy crisis. Such a crisis would arise, for example, if, when first entering China, an MNE relied too much on local leaders and rapidly expanded the local employee base. This shows that MNEs need to pay attention to both economic and social activities to avoid corporate crises and achieve sustainable growth in emerging markets. A study by Darendeli and Hill (2015) came to a similar conclusion. From an analysis of the natural experiment occasioned by the events of the Arab Spring in Libya, they found that MNEs are investing in social welfare projects and having little contact with the Gaddafi clan gained wide legitimacy, thus providing a good example of how to avoid political risks.

Legitimacy is regarded as an important resource for the survival and development of new ventures. Institutional distance directly affects the legitimacy of MNEs' foreign subsidiaries, which is mainly manifested in the fact that when there is a large institutional distance between the home country and the host country, MNEs usually obtain the external legitimacy of foreign subsidiaries through M&As. Eden and Miller (2004) suggested that the larger the institutional distance between the home country and the host country, the more likely an MNE is to use a low ownership strategy to establish legitimacy for its foreign subsidiaries. Chan and Makino (2007) found that MNEs were more inclined to improve the external legitimacy of foreign subsidiaries when investing in host countries with a stable institutional environment than in those with an unstable institutional environment. Furthermore, the empirical study of Meyer et al. (2014) found that Chinese SOEs faced institutional pressure from host countries when setting up foreign subsidiaries in overseas markets because of a belief within some host countries that Chinese SOEs are more likely to threaten their national security and induce unfair competition with support from the Chinese government. This line of thinking makes it harder for Chinese SOEs to gain legitimacy in these markets. To enter foreign markets and gain legitimacy, therefore, Chinese SOEs tend to build new foreign subsidiaries with a low controlling stake instead of choosing an M&A approach. Husted et al. (2016) found that the subsidiaries of MNEs imitated the national certification (such as ISO140001) of geographically close companies to overcome the liability of foreignness. In contrast, domestic companies imitated the global certification of similar companies to overcome the liability of localness.

From the above literature review, it can be seen that the influence of institutions and cultures on MNEs' foreign subsidiaries has mainly been studied through empirical research from the perspective of institutional theory, with the discussion mostly centred on how to gain legitimacy. Consequently, there has been little discussion of the legitimacy construction process and formation mechanism of MNEs' foreign subsidiaries in emerging economies. Nonetheless, there has been some exploration of the factors affecting subsidiary legitimacy, with the research focus shifting from macro-institutional factors to micro-cultural and cognitive factors.

References

Anderson, E., & Gatignon, H. (1986). Modes of foreign entry: A transaction cost analysis and propositions. *Journal of International Business Studies, 17*, 1–26.

Andersson, U., Forsgren, M., & Holm, U. (2002). The strategic impact of external networks: Subsidiary performance and competence development in the multinational corporation. *Strategic Management Journal, 23*(11), 979–996.

Ang, S. H., Benischke, M. H., & Doh, J. P. (2014). The interactions of institutions on foreign market entry mode. *Strategic Management Journal, 36*(10), 1536–1533.

Birkinshaw, J. M., & Morrison, A. J. (1995). Configurations of strategy and structure in subsidiaries of multinational corporations. *Journal of International Business Studies, 26*, 729–753.

Brouthers, K. D., & Hennart, J. F. (2007). Boundaries of the firm: Insights from international entry mode research. *Journal of Management, 33*(3), 395–425.

Cantwell, J. (2009). Location and the multinational enterprise. *Journal of International Business Studies, 40*(1), 35–41.

Chan, C. M., & Makino, S. (2007). Legitimacy and multi-level institutional environments: Implications for foreign subsidiary ownership structure. *Journal of International Business Studies, 38*(4), 621–638.

Chang, E., & Taylor, M. S. (1999). Control in Multinational Corporations (MNCs): The case of Korean manufacturing subsidiaries. *Journal of Management, 25*(4), 541–565.

Chang, Y. Y., Mellahi, K., & Wilkinson, A. (2009). Control of subsidiaries of MNCs from emerging economies in developed countries: The case of

Taiwanese MNCs in the UK. *International Journal of Human Resource Management, 20*(1), 75–95.

Chen, G., Firth, M., & Xu, L. (2009). Does the type of ownership control matter? Evidence from China's listed companies. *Journal of Banking & Finance, 33*(1), 171–181.

Costello, A., & Costello, T. (2010). Aligning the interests of subsidiaries and headquarters in multinational corporations. *Multinational Business Review, 17*(4), 163–204.

Cui, L., & Jiang, F. (2012). State ownership effect on firms' FDI ownership decisions under institutional pressure: A study of Chinese outward-investing firms. *Journal of International Business Studies, 43*(3), 264–284.

Darendeli, I. S., & Hill, T. L. (2015). Uncovering the complex relationships between political risk and MNE firm legitimacy: Insights from Libya. *Journal of International Business Studies, 47*(1), 68–92.

Demirbag, M., Tatoglu, E., & Glaister, K. W. (2009). Equity-based entry modes of emerging country multinationals: Lessons from Turkey. *Journal of World Business, 44*(4), 445–462.

Dimitratos, P., Lioukas, S., Ibeh, K. I. N., & Wheeler, C. (2010). Governance mechanisms of small and medium enterprise international partner management. *British Journal of Management, 21*(3), 754–771.

Donaldson, L., & Davis, J. H. (1994). Boards and company performance—Research challenges the conventional wisdom. *Corporate Governance: An International Review, 2*(3), 151–160.

Du, Y., Deloof, M., & Jorissen, A. (2015). The roles of subsidiary boards in multinational enterprises. *Journal of International Management, 21*(3), 169–181.

Eden, L., & Miller, S. R. (2004). Distance matters: Liability of foreignness, institutional distance and ownership strategy. *Advances in International Management, 16*, 187–221.

Erramilli, M. K., & Rao, C. P. (1993). Service firms' international entry-mode choice: A modified transaction-cost analysis approach. *The Journal of Marketing, 57*(3), 19–38.

Fey, C. F., & Furu, P. (2008). Top management incentive compensation and knowledge sharing in multinational corporations. *Strategic Management Journal, 29*(12), 1301–1323.

Filatotchev, I., Stephan, J., & Jindra, B. (2008). Ownership structure, strategic controls and export intensity of foreign-invested firms in transition economies. *Journal of International Business Studies, 39*(7), 1133–1148.

Finkelstein, S., & Hambrick, D. C. (1996). *Strategic leadership: Top executives and their effects on organisations*. South-Western Pub.

Ghoshal, S., & Bartlett, C. A. (1990). The multinational corporation as an interorganizational network. *Academy of Management Review, 15(4)*, 603–625.

Gong, Y. (2006). The impact of subsidiary top management team national diversity on subsidiary performance: Knowledge and legitimacy perspectives. *Management International Review, 46(6)*, 771–790.

Gupta, A. K., & Govindarajan, V. (2000). Knowledge flows within multinational corporations. *Strategic Management Journal, 21(4)*, 473–496.

Hambrick, D. C., & Mason, P. A. (1984). Upper echelons: The organisation as a reflection of its top managers. *Academy of Management Review, 9(2)*, 193–206.

Herrmann, P., & Datta, D. K. (2005). Relationships between top management team characteristics and international diversification: An empirical investigation. *British Journal of Management, 16(1)*, 69–78.

Husted, B. W., Montiel, I., & Christmann, P. (2016). Effects of local legitimacy on certification decisions to global and national CSR standards by multinational subsidiaries and domestic firms. *Journal of International Business Studies, 47*, 328–396.

Jensen, M. C., & Meckling, W. H. (1976). Theory of the firm: Managerial behaviour, agency costs and ownership structure. *Journal of Financial Economics, 3(4)*, 305–360.

Kiel, G. C., Hendry, K., & Nicholson, G. J. (2006). Corporate governance options for the local subsidiaries of multinational enterprises. *Corporate Governance: An International Review, 14(6)*, 568–576.

Kim, B., Prescott, J. E., & Kim, S. M. (2005). Differentiated governance of foreign subsidiaries in multinational corporations: An agency theory perspective. *Journal of International Management, 11(1)*, 43–66.

Kor, Y. Y. (2006). Direct and interaction effects of top management team and board compositions on R&D investment strategy. *Strategic Management Journal, 27(11)*, 1081–1099.

Kostova, T. (1999). Multinational transfer of strategic organisational practices: A contextual perspective [J]. *Academy of Management Review, 24*, 308–324.

Kostova, T., & Roth, K. (2002). Adoption of an organisational practice by subsidiaries of multinational corporations: institutional and relational effects. *Academy of Management Journal, 45(1)*, 215–233.

Kostova, T., Roth, K., & Dacin, M. T. (2008). Institutional theory in the study of multinational corporations: A critique and new directions. *Academy of Management Review, 33(4)*, 994–1006.

Kriger, M. P. (1988). The increasing role of subsidiary boards in MNCs: An empirical study. *Strategic Management Journal, 9(4)*, 347–360.

Kwok, C. C. Y., & Tadesse, S. (2006). The MNC as an agent of change for host-country institutions: FDI and corruption. *Journal of International Business Studies, 37*(6), 767–785.

Li, W. A. (2009). *Corporate governance* (2nd ed.). Higher Education Press.

Liang, H., Ren, B., & Sun, S. L. (2015). An anatomy of state control in the globalisation of state-owned enterprises. *Journal of International Business Studies, 46*(2), 223–240.

Lin, R. H., Zhang, H. J., Fan, J. H., & Shuai, Y. X. (2009). Research on network governance evaluation of enterprise groups: A case study based on Acer. *Review of Corporate Governance, 1*(4), 29–44.

Luo, Y., & Tung, R. L. (2007). International expansion of emerging market enterprises: A springboard perspective. *Journal of International Business Studies, 38*(4), 481–498.

Meyer, K. E., Ding, Y., Li, J., & Zhang, H. (2014). Overcoming distrust: How state-owned enterprises adapt their foreign entries to institutional pressures abroad. *Journal of International Business Studies, 45*(8), 1005–1028.

Meyer, K. E., Mudambi, R., & Narula, R. (2011). Multinational enterprises and local contexts: The opportunities and challenges of multiple embeddedness. *Journal of Management Studies, 48*(2), 235–252.

Monteiro, L. F., Arvidsson, N., & Birkinshaw, J. (2008). Knowledge flows within multinational corporations: Explaining subsidiary isolation and its performance implications. *Organisation Science, 19*(1), 90–107.

O'Donnell, S. W. (2000). Managing foreign subsidiaries: Agents of headquarters, or an interdependent network? *Strategic Management Journal, 21*(5), 525–548.

Pan, Y., Teng, L., Supapol, A. B., Lu, X., Huang, D., & Wang, Z. (2014). Firms' FDI ownership: The influence of government ownership and legislative connections. *Journal of International Business Studies, 45*(8), 1029–1043.

Rosenzweig, P. M., & Singh, J. V. (1991). Organizational environments and the multinational enterprise. *Academy of Management Review, 16*(2), 340–361.

Roth, K., & Morrison, A. J. (1992). Implementing global strategy: Characteristics of global subsidiary mandates. *Journal of International Business Studies, 23*, 715–735.

Sekiguchi, T., Bebenroth, R., & Li, D. (2011). Nationality background of MNC affiliates' top management and affiliate performance in Japan: Knowledge-based and upper echelons perspectives. *International Journal of Human Resource Management, 22*(05), 999–1016.

Woodcock, C. P., Beamish, P. W., & Makino, S. (1994). Ownership-based entry mode strategies and international performance. *Journal of International Business Studies, 25*, 253–273.

Xie, Q. (2014). CEO Tenure and ownership mode choice of Chinese firms: The moderating roles of managerial discretion. *International Business Review, 23*(5), 910–919.

Xu, D., & Shenkar, O. (2002). Note: Institutional distance and the multinational enterprise. *Academy of Management Review, 27*(4), 608–618.

Yan, G. H., Yuan, H. L., & Lin, M. (2004). Governance and control of overseas enterprises from the perspective of knowledge. *Contemporary Finance & Economics, 2004*(2), 67–70.

Zhao, M., Park, S. H., & Zhou, N. (2014). MNC strategy and social adaptation in emerging markets. *Journal of International Business Studies, 45*(7), 842–861.

CHAPTER 6

Institutional Distance, Cultural Distance, and MNEs Governance

6.1 Factors Influencing MNEs Governance

With the rapid development of the global economy, MNEs are constantly seeking new markets. It has become a common practice to invest directly in overseas markets by setting up foreign subsidiaries, in the process of which many important strategic decisions must be made. Understanding the factors that influence decision-making in multinational investment, such as the choice of entry mode and host country and the need to address legitimacy problems, is crucial because these also constitute the influencing factors of MNE governance. According to Meyer et al. (2011), a foreign subsidiary is externally embedded in the local environment (the host country's institutional environment, politics, economy, and culture) and internally embedded in the MNE environment (the parent company's goals, strategies, and corporate governance). Moreover, the meso-environment of MNEs also has a significant impact on the governance of MNEs.

Each of the factors affecting the governance of an MNE can be classified as belonging to one of three environments: the national environment at the macro-level, including the institutional environment, law, politics, economy, cultures, and national risks of the home country and host countries, as well as the institutional, economic, cultural, psychic, and geographical distance between the home and host countries; the competitive environment of the relevant industry at the meso-level, with varying

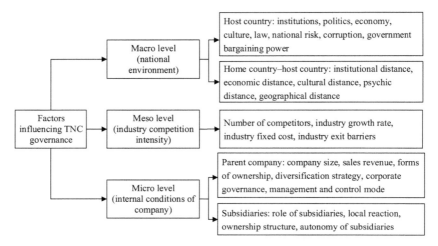

Fig. 6.1 Framework of factors influencing MNE governance

levels of intensity depending on such factors as the number of competitors, industry growth rate, industry fixed costs, and industry exit barriers; and the parent company's internal conditions at the micro-level, including the goals, strategies, and corporate governance of the parent company (Fig. 6.1).

6.1.1 Influencing Factors of MNEs Governance at the Macro Level

In a study of the influencing factors of MNE governance at the macro level, Erramilli and Rao (1993) verified the influence of national characteristics resulting from the combination of cultural and economic factors on the ownership of foreign subsidiaries. Rodriguez et al. (2005) analysed the relationship between government corruption and MNEs' entry strategies using institutional theory. The influence of the distance between the home and host countries on the governance of MNEs has also been studied by different scholars from different angles.

In terms of institutional distance, Grewal and Dharwadkar (2002) used an institutional theory framework to study the role of three dimensions of institutional environment on marketing channels: regulatory institutions, normative institutions, and cognitive institutions. They suggested that the regulatory institutions of the host country might provide incentives for enterprises in the selection of entry modes. Ando (2012) verified how the institutional distance between the home and host countries affected the ownership structure of foreign subsidiaries. The empirical analysis of a sample of foreign subsidiaries of Japanese companies revealed that the equity ownership ratio of foreign subsidiaries decreased with an increase in institutional distance. Therefore, it can be concluded that in direct overseas investment, the institutional distance between the host and home countries also affects the equity entry mode decision of foreign subsidiaries.

Fisher et al. (2014) introduced the concept of 'economic distance' for trade cost measurement to indicate the degree of market opening and trade facilitation between two countries. A smaller economic distance between two countries is associated with fewer trade obstacles, closer trade relations, and more extensive trade cooperation between the two countries under the condition of lower trading costs.

Ionascu et al. (2004) held that higher cultural distances on the normative and cognitive dimensions would encourage MNEs to enter a host country through M&As to facilitate multinational communication. Yin et al. (2013) found that cultural distance directly affected the performance of Chinese MNEs and that this effect varied according to different performance goals.

Johanson and Wiedersheim-Paul (1975) argued that psychic distance interferes with the flow of information in specific markets, which impedes enterprises from identifying business opportunities in other markets effectively and prevents them from seizing favourable opportunities immediately or extends the time needed to identify such opportunities.

Geographical distance causes information asymmetry (Grote & Rucker, 2007; Ragozzino & Reuer, 2009), which is a key reason for the failure of cross-border M&As. Jia et al. (2005) used a sample of 524 overseas M&As by Chinese enterprises to examine the influence of experience on cross-border M&As initiated by MNEs in developing countries and the moderating effect of geographical distance and state-owned equity. They found a positive U-shaped relationship between experience and the success rate of cross-border M&As, and that geographical distance not only directly reduced the success rate of M&As but also negatively moderated the relationship between experience and the success rate of cross-border M&As.

6.1.2 Influencing Factors of MNEs Governance at the Meso-Level

Lecraw (1984) analysed the relationship between the bargaining power, ownership, and profitability of MNEs using four main determinants of MNEs' equity ownership level in subsidiaries: the desired level of equity ownership of MNEs and their subsidiaries, the bargaining power of MNEs, the desired level of equity ownership of local shareholding enterprises in host countries, and the bargaining power of host governments. The study also considered the influence of industry competitors on the equity ownership of subsidiaries. The findings suggest that over time, the actual equity ownership held by MNEs decreases as the attractiveness of the host country weakens and the number of potential multinational investors increases. However, few studies have examined the influencing factors of MNEs governance at the meso-level, and most of these have treated these factors (such as the type of industry, the number of competitors, and the growth rate of the industry) as control variables.

6.1.3 Influencing Factors of MNEs Governance at the Micro-Level

Fagre and Wells (1982) were among the first to study the influencing factors of MNE governance at the micro-level, and they concluded that equity ownership is the result of negotiation between MNEs and host countries and is thus determined by the bargaining position of both parties. Anderson and Gatignon (1986) studied the choice of foreign market entry mode based on the transaction cost theory. Their findings suggest that a higher degree of control is more suitable for those entrants with closely coordinated global strategies. Delios and Henisz (2000) found that in countries at high risk of public expropriation hazards, the importance of experience tended to replace that of the local knowledge of host countries and the political market provided by local partners, thus mitigating public expropriation hazards. As a result, the negative effect of public expropriation hazards on the level of equity ownership of a subsidiary in a given country is smaller in magnitude for foreign investing firms with greater (host country/industry/international) experience; in contrast, for investments at high risk of private expropriation hazards, experience tended to facilitate the preparation, monitoring, and execution of contracts and help to screen partners, and provide the multinational with the capability to reduce the expected variance in opportunistic behaviour by a potential joint venture partner, thus reducing the positive effect of private expropriation hazards on the level of equity ownership of a subsidiary in a given country.

In research related to enterprise internationalisation, scholars in various disciplinary contexts have outlined and verified the effects of different types of distance, including geographical, economic, administrative (Ghemawat, 2001), institutional (Kostova & Roth, 2002), and linguistic distance. Institutional and cultural distances remain the most widely studied types of distance in international business research (Beugelsdijk & Mudambi, 2013; Shenkar et al., 2008). Van Hoorn and Maseland (2016) pointed out that institutional distance has become an increasingly popular research perspective for studying enterprises' multinational investment and management behaviour. Similarly, in a review of Hofstede-inspired research, Kirkman et al. (2006) concluded that most studies had examined the impact of cultural distance on organisational and country-level outcomes. Lopez-Duarte et al. (2016) found that more than 80% of the literature on culture and firm internationalisation was focused on cultural distance.

This chapter places more emphasis on the influencing factors of MNE governance at the macro-level, especially on the influence of the institutional and cultural distance between the home and host countries at the macro-level (the national environment). The impact of these two types of distance on the governance of MNEs is discussed in the following two sections.

6.2 Institutional Distance and MNEs Governance

Research probing into international business and business strategies based on the concept of institutional distance appeared in the literature as early as the 1990s, and studies on international business and strategies from the institution-based view emerged in large numbers in the early twenty-first century (Peng, 2003). There is now an abundance of research results on the topic of institutional distance. Given that they operate in different countries or regions, MNEs are subject to institutional distance resulting from cultural and institutional differences. Hofstede (1980) analysed the differences between countries from the perspective of cultural value and put forward the concept of 'cultural distance', which laid the foundation for conceptualising and research into the institutional distance.

North (1990) distinguished between formal and informal types of institutions. Kostova (1999) proposed the concept of 'institutional distance' to refer to the extent of similarity or dissimilarity between the normative, cognitive, and standard institutions of a pair of countries. Following Scott's (1995) three dimensions of the institution (regulatory, normative, and cognitive), institutional distance is further defined as the differences between countries in regulatory, normative, and cognitive systems. Kostova and Zaheer (1999) used the country institutional profile (CIP) to measure a country's institutional characteristics in each of these three dimensions and regarded institutional distance as the differences in institutional profile between the home and host countries. Also, based on Scott's definition of institution, Kaufmann et al. (2010) constructed a set of indicators to measure the differences in normative and regulatory institutions between two countries. Regulatory institutions refer to the existing laws and regulations of a country, and normative institutions refer to the beliefs, values, and moral norms rooted in society and the specific ways of thinking, understanding, and expressing problems. Regulatory institutions reflect the rights of citizens to carry out social and economic activities, while normative institutions define the nature of citizens' activities and their judgements on their ability to act (Eden & Miller, 2004).

6.2.1   *Institutional Distance and Host Country Selection*

The institutional environment is a key factor in a country's economic performance. In countries that lack sound institutional mechanisms and effective law enforcement, the government often subjects foreign companies to 'institutional predation' by collecting economic rent on administrative grounds. For the sake of relationship maintenance and survival, foreign companies often seek the shelter of official powers through illegitimate means, such as bribery, or shift the costs to the public and thus undermine national well-being. Meanwhile, FDI location choices are affected by 'institutional proximity' (Habib & Zurawicki, 2002). Countries with sound institutions and laws and similar beliefs to the home country are usually preferred. The countries receiving the investment also show obvious biases in their attitudes towards FDI: in particular, countries that have been invaded or colonised in the past take a more cautious and defensive attitude towards the inflow of FDI, fearing that it may represent 'economic colonialism' and pose a threat to state sovereignty and national culture.

To set up subsidiaries in a host country, an MNE must be accepted within the local environment and gain legitimacy by acquiring necessary resources. The successful acquisition of these resources depends on the practical activities carried out by the organisation. Therefore, there is an interactive relationship between organisational practices and the choice of the institutional environment. To survive and develop, organisations must actively cope with institutional and competitive pressures, and this coping behaviour deepens the similarities and differences between organisations in outcomes and behaviour. From the perspective of organisational theory, to survive and develop in a particular environment, an organisation must obtain the necessary resources and support from the environment and consider what is required within the institutional environment to fit in and be recognised. Therefore, an enterprise's behaviour reflects its adaptation to the institutional environment to a certain extent, which is an essential factor affecting the selection of host countries by MNEs.

Davis and North (1971) was the first scholar to explain the market operation mechanism using institutional factors, which later became a popular approach to analysing FDI location selection. Many scholars have since shown that a sound and the efficient institutional system helps to reduce transaction costs and to promote the effective allocation of resources (Kaufmann et al., 2009). In contrast, a poor institutional environment increases transaction costs and weakens the host country's ability to attract FDI. FDI by MNEs incurs high sunk costs, but in the long run, a stable political environment and high contract execution efficiency in a host country can offset the extra sunk costs attributed to uncertainty. Institutions constitute the rules and norms for social activities (North, 1990) or the 'cognitive, normative, and regulative structures and activities that provide stability and meaning to social activities' (Scott, 1995, 33). Economic organisations always operate in a specific institutional environment, and their economic behaviour is restricted by the rules system prevailing within this environment, leading to institutional isomorphism within the system (Dacin, 1997). Therefore, the institutional environment is an important factor in corporate behaviour. As the institutional environment of each country is unique, for multinational investment and operations, MNEs must not only adapt to different institutional environments but must also deal with the risks and pressures associated with operating in different institutional environments. Such is the influence of institutional distance on the multinational operations.

FDI by MNEs in a host country at a long institutional distance from the home country is subject to risks associated with the differences in regulatory institutions, such as the judicial arbitration mechanism and contractual guarantees, between the two countries. Habib and Zurawicki (2002) held that when studying FDI decision-making and the institutional quality and environment of the host country, we should also consider the institutional distance: the differences in the institutional quality and environment between the host and home countries. MNEs are more willing to invest in host countries with institutions and cultures similar to those of their home countries, as this can reduce the uncertainties involved in their operations. Xu and Shenkar (2002) theorised the relationship between institutional distance and MNEs' location selection as follows: MNEs with long-term global strategies prefer host countries at a short institutional distance from the home country, whereas MNEs that implement multinational and localisation strategies favour host countries at a long institutional distance from the home country. A greater institutional distance is associated with higher fixed costs for overseas operations.

The institutional differences between countries are bound to affect the choice of host countries for foreign subsidiaries. Meyer (2001) studied the entry mode selection of MNEs from the UK and Germany when they entered Eastern European countries undergoing an institutional transition from centrally planned to market economies. From the perspective of transaction costs, Meyer analysed what entry strategies MNEs should adopt if they adapted to local institutions and probed into the relationships between different institutions, the internationalisation of management, and technological knowledge. The results showed that German entrants were more likely to establish wholly-owned subsidiaries because of Germany's geographical proximity to Eastern Europe compared with the UK. Cantwell (2009) studied the selection of location for MNE subsidiaries and found that when seeking the locational composition of the international network of resources, MNEs often refer to the institutional compatibility of the location with their own, which influences the local institutional environment. As can be seen from the above, the institutional environment of the host country determines the institutional distance between the host and home countries and affects the choice of host countries for foreign subsidiaries.

Moreover, some scholars believe that MNEs try to establish a competitive edge in host countries by either transferring advantages from the parent company or cultivating unique capabilities in subsidiaries in overseas business operations, for which institutional distance is a key factor in the competitiveness of MNEs in foreign markets. When an MNE intends to transfer the advantages of the parent company to its subsidiaries, countries at a short institutional distance from the home country are more suitable. In contrast, when an MNE intends to cultivate unique capabilities in its subsidiaries, countries at a long institutional distance from the home country are more suitable.

6.2.2 Institutional Distance and Choice of Entry Mode by Foreign Subsidiaries

Scholars in China and abroad have studied the influence of institutional distance on the ownership entry mode of foreign subsidiaries from different angles. Studies have examined the choice of entry modes by enterprises for cross-regional direct investment mainly from the perspective of transaction cost theory or internalisation. Over the past dozen years, some scholars have also adopted the cultural and institutional perspectives to study entry mode decisions. In China, the government plays an essential role in both politics and the economy, so the institutional theory is more relevant for research on Chinese enterprise behaviours.

Meyer (2001) studied the entry mode selection of MNEs from the UK and Germany when they entered Eastern European countries that were undergoing an institutional transformation from a centrally planned to a market economy. From the perspective of transaction costs, Meyer's study analysed what entry strategies MNEs should adopt if they are to adapt to local institutions and probed into the relationships between different institutions, the internationalisation of the management, and technological knowledge. The results showed that foreign investors had a stronger preference for internationalisation and were more likely to establish wholly-owned subsidiaries in countries with advanced institutional development. Scott (1995), a representative of institutional theory in organisational sociology, divided institutional constraints into formal and informal and categorised institutions as regulatory, normative, and cognitive. In their research into institutional distance and MNEs, Xu and Shenkar (2002) used the same regulatory, normative, and cognitive dimensions to categorise types of the institutional distance between the host and home countries. They studied MNEs' choices of host countries and the factors influencing foreign market entry strategies based on the matching degree between the three dimensions and various enterprise attributes. The institutional distance proposed in their study complements the concept of cultural distance and broadens the perspective of strategic countermeasures in MNE theories. Institutional distance in a broad sense includes cultural distance and serves as the foundation for studying the relationships between institutional distance, cultural distance, and MNE governance.

Among relevant empirical studies, Peng (2003) explained how organisations made strategic choices during fundamental institutional transitions. Peng proposed two strategies corresponding to two phases of institutional transition: a network-centred strategy adopted under the relationship-based personalised transaction structure and a market-centred strategy adopted under a rule-based impersonalised exchange regime. The strategic choices made by overseas entrants under institutional pressure were also analysed. The study found that in economies with poor or inadequate formal institutions, overseas entrants tended to adopt a network-based strategy emphasising informal interpersonal relationships to enter the foreign market by allying with local companies or establishing joint ventures. In contrast, in economies with sound formal institutions, MNEs were more likely to enter the foreign market by establishing wholly-owned subsidiaries or acquiring local enterprises. Doh et al. (2003) adopted a research framework incorporating two basic dimensions (pervasiveness and arbitrariness) of government corruption for an empirical study based on 220 projects in 64 emerging countries. They proposed five strategies that MNEs should consider in dealing with corruption when investing in foreign markets. The results show that, in general, a higher level of corruption in host countries was associated with a higher likelihood of foreign entrants choosing joint ventures rather than establishing wholly-owned subsidiaries. The study suggests that the level of corruption was an important factor affecting institutional distance, so the results reflect the relationship between institutional distance and equity entry mode. All of these empirical studies considered the influence of institutions on MNEs' foreign market entry mode, but they did not take sufficient account of the institutional distance between the home and host countries; thus, further study is needed.

In analysing the entry strategies of foreign investors entering emerging economies, Meyer et al. (2009) advanced the institution-based view of entry strategies by integrating it with the resource-based view and applied it to verify the influence of market-supporting institutions on corporate strategies. They argued that MNEs would be more inclined to acquire resources through joint ventures when entering emerging economies with weak market-supporting institutions. However, when entering emerging economies with strong market-supporting institutions, this tendency would decrease because acquisitions play an important role in accessing intangible resources. By taking into account the degree of institutionalisation, the study of Meyer et al. reflects a certain extent the directionality of institutional distance but not its magnitude. Moreover, although the authors classified the entry strategies into joint ventures, acquisitions, and greenfield investment, these three strategies were not clearly defined.

In terms of entry mode selection in multinational investment, Polesello et al. (2013) examined the influencing factors with a case study of WEG, a Brazilian motor manufacturer operating in several host countries, including Argentina, Portugal, Austria, India, Mexico, the United States, and China. The study explores the influence of resources, industry, and institutional environment on entry mode selection during FDI activities. Anil et al. (2014) conducted an empirical study on a sample of Turkish MNEs that undertook FDI in Romania to investigate the ownership and market entry mode of MNEs in emerging economies. The study made a detailed analysis of interview data from an institutional perspective and revealed different impacts of the risks and uncertainty in the host country on the decision-making of different foreign investors. Hernández and Nieto (2015) analysed the effects of the positions of the home and host countries, with different positions exerting an asymmetric effect of institutional distance on the entry mode. Using a sample of European enterprises, the results showed that when the regulatory development level of the host country was lower than that of the home country, MNEs chose entry modes requiring low resource commitment; otherwise, enterprises chose entry modes requiring high resource commitment. The findings also revealed that the direction of regulatory institutional distance had a significant influence on the entry mode choice of enterprises.

6.2.3 Institutional Distance and the Legitimacy of Foreign Subsidiaries

The legitimacy of an entity refers to whether its actions are desirable, proper, or appropriate within some socially constructed system of norms, values, beliefs, and definitions. Whether an organisation is legitimate is determined by the common norms, values, standards, and social expectations that are recognised and followed by the stakeholders in the area of its operation.

Research on organisational legitimacy, especially on the legitimacy of MNEs, has been mainly based on institutional theory and has emphasised the role of the institutional environment within which enterprises are embedded while analysing the influence of cultural distance and institutional distance on their strategies. The research findings suggest that MNEs should adapt to the complex institutional environments of both the home and host countries and make strategic decisions (such as entry mode choices) corresponding to the need to fit into the host country environment and enhance their legitimacy. Meyer and Peng (2005) and Kostova et al. (2008) argued that institutional theory should be combined with other theories for studying the multinational operation of MNEs. In a study of Chinese MNEs, Luo and Tung (2007) found that the adaptability (in terms of the achievement of legitimacy) of foreign subsidiaries to the market of their host countries was directly related to the host country environment and the international experience of and capital owned by the MNEs. Institutional theory is mainly concerned with the influence of the external environment on the legitimacy of MNEs (Kostova & Zaheer, 1999) and emphasises their adaptability to the external environment. Social capital theory, in contrast, stresses the initiative of enterprises in gaining and enhancing legitimacy, proposing that enterprises can build and increase their legitimacy by expanding their social capital. As an important theoretical basis for studying the strategic choices of MNEs, institutional theory suggests that MNEs must adapt to the external environment and the rules of the system to survive and develop (Meyer & Rowan, 1977; Scott, 1995). Cross-country operations make it difficult for MNEs to establish and maintain legitimacy, as they have to cope with different institutional environments and different perceptions of organisational legitimacy (Kostova & Zaheer, 1999). MNEs need to adapt to the institutional environments of both the home and host countries by dealing with similarities and dissimilarities in institutions (Chan et al., 2008; Kostova & Roth, 2002), which brings forth unique opportunities and challenges for foreign subsidiaries (Tan, 2009).

Scott (1995) and Kostova (1996) introduced institutional distance as a new perspective for studying the behaviour of MNEs. They believed that greater institutional distance would make it more difficult for MNEs to establish legitimacy in the host country and transfer their strategies and rules to foreign subsidiaries. In other words, a long institutional distance triggers a conflict in foreign subsidiaries between the need to attain external legitimacy (a positive local response) in the host country and the MNE's demands for internal consistency (or global integration). Therefore, it can be concluded that institutional distance affects the strategic choices of enterprises.

Institutional distance also affects enterprises' choices between establishing new subsidiaries or taking an M&A approach to cross-regional direct investment. This is supported by empirical evidence suggesting that when national differences are apparent, MNEs tend to build a new enterprise instead of acquiring an existing one because these differences can amplify the problems involved in the implementation of M&As. Kostova (1999) held that long institutional distance hinders the transfer of organisational practices from the parent company to subsidiaries. Just as it is difficult to impose internal consistency on an acquired subsidiary, competitive advantages cannot be simply copied across. Local players have formed their common practices in the host country environment. Therefore, it is difficult for an acquired subsidiary to obtain legitimacy from within the enterprise in the context of significant institutional disparity. On the contrary, a newly established subsidiary may be regarded as a descendant of the MNE. Compared with subsidiaries created via the acquisition of local firms, greenfield investment is more acceptable for maintaining compliance with the parent company's rules and regulations. Therefore, to avoid conflicts within the organisation and difficulties in integrating foreign subsidiaries, MNEs tend to choose greenfield investment when entering new markets with a long institutional distance from their home markets.

6.3 Cultural Distance and MNEs Governance

Culture is the operational paradigm of thinking (Hofstede, 1980) and has the attribute of cognitive thinking (Hofstede & Bond, 1988). Hofstede, a Dutch scholar, put forward the widely accepted claim that organisational culture has a major influence on management decision-making. He defined four cultural dimensions that affect management activities or management decision-making styles: individualism/collectivism, power distance, uncertainty avoidance, and masculinity/femininity. According to this four-dimensional view of culture, social values (individualism/collectivism) and social behaviour codes (power distance) are the embodiment of cultural characteristics, such that culture takes on the quality of social norms (Eden & Miller, 2004). In addition, Hofstede's five-dimensional scale of cultural values, which adds long-term/short-term orientation to the above four dimensions of culture, makes a practical framework for measuring cultural differences between and value orientations within different countries.

Power distance refers to the extent to which a society accepts the unequal distribution of power in an organisation. In high power-distance culture, subordinates are very much dependent on their superiors, and the ideal boss is imagined as an enlightened despot and a merciful dictator; in low power-distance culture, employees are highly involved in decision-making, and subordinates enjoy a certain autonomy with which to carry out their prescribed responsibilities. Individualism indicates a loose social structure in which people primarily care about themselves and their immediate families; collectivism describes a well-connected social structure in which people are divided into in-groups and out-groups, expecting support from and pledging absolute loyalty to their in-groups. Uncertainty avoidance refers to the degree to which a society feels threatened in the face of uncertainty and ambiguity and tries to avoid these by guaranteeing job security, creating more formal rules, rejecting deviant views and types of behaviour, and relying on absolute loyalty and professional knowledge. Masculinity and femininity refer to the degree of dominance of 'male' values in a society—assertiveness, the pursuit of wealth and material rewards, indifference to others, and a focus on the quality of personal life—as opposed to the dominance of 'female' values. Long-term and short-term orientation indicates the extent to which a society values long-term and short-term interests.

Cultural distance describes the cultural differences between different nationalities or countries, rather than emphasising the differences in individual cognitive thinking as in psychic distance (Sousa & Bradley, 2006). Kogut and Singh (1988) put forward a model for calculating the cultural distance that has been widely used in subsequent studies. In multinational operations, MNEs try to meet the rent-seeking demands in the host country market by communicating and negotiating with the administrative agencies of the host country in a way that is generally accepted locally to maintain their economic or commercial interests. Suppose there are substantial differences in normative institutions between the home and host countries, such as differences in cultural patterns and social norms. In that case, there is a higher probability of failure in cross-cultural communication between MNEs, subsidiaries in the host country, and host country customers, which increase the costs and risks of the multinational operation. Lorre and Guisinger (1995) found that normative institutional differences, such as those captured by cultural differences, were important factors affecting the FDI of US enterprises. In view of the above, this section introduces the influence of cultural distance on three internationalisation outcomes: the choice of entry mode, the choice of the host country, and the attainment of legitimacy by foreign subsidiaries of MNEs.

6.3.1 Cultural Distance and the Choice of Host Country

The concept of location advantage was put forward in the eclectic paradigm of international production by Dunning (1988), who explained the flow direction of FDI based on the location advantage of the host country. Dunning classified location factors into four categories: market factors, trade barriers, cost factors, and aspects of the investment environment. In addition, he held that psychic distance, which addresses aspects of language, culture, and habit, affected the location choice of FDI. The location choice of FDI has since attracted the increasing attention of scholars, with culture included as a factor affecting location choice.

When transaction costs are used to explain FDI location choice, minimising the costs becomes the primary goal of MNEs in investment decision-making. From this perspective, the greater the cultural difference, the higher the costs of FDI. Empirical studies have shown a negative correlation between cultural differences and direct investment (Grosse & Trevino, 1996): the larger the cultural differences between the home and host countries, the less direct investment the host country can attract. However, there is no consensus on the influence of cultural differences on international direct investment in academic circles. Veugelers (1991) used language to represent cultural similarity and found that this variable was one of the most important factors affecting FDI distribution within OECD member countries. Lorre and Guisinger (1995) found that normative institutional differences, such as those captured by cultural difference, were important factors affecting the FDI of American enterprises. This view was supported by the study of Li and Guisinger (1992). There are many explanations for this finding. As global economic integration progresses, countries become more closely interconnected in such areas as training and communication, resulting in fewer cultural differences. Thomas and Grosse (2001) found a positive correlation between cultural differences and inward direct investments in Mexico. Although the authors did not provide a reasonable explanation, their findings corroborate the notion of a change in the role of cultural difference in FDI. Thomas and Grosse (2001) believed that national cultural factors played an important role in the introduction of FDI in developing countries.

Based on case studies of several Swedish MNEs, Shleifer and Robert (1993) and Johanson and Vahlne (2009) put forward the concept of 'psychic distance', analogous to 'geographical distance'. The psychic distance between the host and home countries has a major influence on FDI location choice. MNEs are often affected by psychic distance when entering foreign markets, which impedes the information exchange between MNEs and the host country market. In addition, the psychic distance affects multinational operation costs, which influence the location choice of FDI. Therefore, MNEs generally prefer a shorter psychic distance. For example, MNEs in Sweden prefer Denmark, Norway, and Finland as their overseas target markets.

All of the abovementioned influences on FDI—of cultural patterns, national cultural factors, and psychic distance—reflect the relevance of cultural distance to the choice of the host country or business location.

6.3.2 Cultural Distance and the Choice of Foreign Market Entry Mode

For enterprises to overcome the obstacles to operating in overseas markets posed by cultural differences between countries (i.e. cultural distance), they need to adjust their degree of ownership of overseas subsidiaries accordingly. Cultural distance increases the difficulty for host country employees to understand and accept the culture of the home country, which may lead to internal conflicts. Partnering with local businesses is an effective way for MNEs to solve such conflicts. The greater the cultural distance, and thus the higher the potential for cultural conflict, the greater is the ownership stake allocated to local partners in exchange for additional support. A well-functioning governance structure is a key to the proper operation of enterprises. However, cultural distance adds to the complexity of MNE governance, increasing the burden of international operations. Cooperating with local partners helps enterprises identify various stakeholders' demands and reduce governance complexity but requesting more help from local partners entails giving them a higher equity stake.

Cultural distance aggravates the liability of foreignness and the difficulties faced by MNEs operating in a foreign country, thus placing them in an unfavourable position when competing with host country enterprises (Zaheer, 1995). Cultural differences can also make it harder for MNEs to understand consumer habits and behaviour in the host country. Greater cultural distance brings higher costs for enterprises to understand the market and consumer behaviour in the host country. MNEs, therefore, turn to local partners to attain such an understanding. By reducing investment intensity and equity control, MNEs can receive more resource support from local partners to leverage local partners' insights into the local culture and thus avoid the uncertainties arising from differences in cultural values and reduce overseas investment risk.

A further problem associated with cultural distance is that it makes it more difficult for MNEs to understand and communicate with their partners and therefore limits the accuracy of predicting the speculative behaviour of the partners, which increases investment risk (Chang et al., 2012). Enterprises then need to expend significant time and energy to supervise their partners' behaviour to reduce the risks from speculation associated with their partners, which adds to operation and management costs. In addition, after establishing a subsidiary overseas, MNEs need to transfer the management and operations knowledge and core competitiveness of the parent company to the subsidiary company. However, the greater the cultural distance between the two countries, the greater the difference between the parent company and the subsidiary in the operations and management backgrounds and the cultural paradigms and values followed by the employees. These differences make communication and understanding between the employees of the two countries more difficult (Luo, 2009), thus significantly increasing the cost of knowledge transfer from the parent company to the subsidiary and the management costs involved in this transfer. An MNE with a high equity ownership stake can transfer its knowledge, experience, and core competitiveness to its subsidiaries more easily. Moreover, a higher investment ratio gives the parent company greater decision-making power and higher efficiency (Jia, 2008).

Ionascu et al. (2004) argued that when faced with normative and cognitive distance, MNEs prefer to enter the host country market through M&As to facilitate cross-border communication. According to research by Chen and Fan (2013) that considered normative distance and cognitive distance (including cultural distance), MNEs that are eager to gain legitimacy in the host country generally prefer M&As to greenfield investment, as the takeover of existing businesses can produce legitimacy spillover. However, post-merger integration issues become prominent in the regulatory environment in the short term, which makes it less likely for Chinese MNEs to choose M&As.

6.3.3 *Cultural Distance and the Legitimacy of Foreign Subsidiaries*

Research on the legitimacy of MNEs has been mainly based on the institutional theory. Therefore, it has emphasised the role of the institutional environment in which the enterprises are embedded and analysed the influence of cultural distance and institutional distance on their strategies. According to the findings of these studies, MNEs should adapt to the complex institutional environments of the home and host countries and make strategic decisions (such as the choice of entry mode) corresponding to the need to adapt to the host country environment and improve their legitimacy.

The complexity of environmental differences between countries means they cannot be fully captured by analyses of the institutional environment (Xu & Shenkar, 2002) or the institutional differences between the home and host country (Kostova, 1996; Scott, 1995). A measurement of cultural distance based on the classification of cultural environments (Hofstede, 1980; Kogut & Singh, 1988) is also needed. The social environment of the host country is the source of the strongest moral and value factors, which makes social legitimacy even harder to achieve for

MNEs than market legitimacy because their outsider identity must be internalised. Cultural distance significantly impacts legitimacy building because it presents as a major barrier for MNEs to be recognised and accepted by the local society. The greater the cultural distance, the more difficult it is to obtain local legitimacy.

REFERENCES

Anderson, E., & Gatignon, H. (1986). Modes of foreign entry: A transaction cost analysis and propositions [J]. *Journal of International Business Studies, 17*(3), 1–26.

Ando, N. (2012). The ownership structure of foreign subsidiaries and the effect of institutional distance: A case study of Japanese firms [J]. *Asia Pacific Business Review, 18*(2), 259–274.

Anil, I., Tatoglu, E., & Ozkasap, G. (2014). Ownership and market entry mode choices of emerging country multinationals in a transition country: Evidence from Turkish multinationals in Romania [J]. *Journal for East European Management Studies, 19*(4), 413–452.

Beugelsdijk, S., & Mudambi, R. (2013). MNEs as border-crossing multi-location enterprises: The role of discontinuities in geographic space [J]. *Journal of International Business Studies, 44*, 413–426.

Cantwell, J. (2009). Location and the multinational enterprise [J]. *Journal of International Business Studies, 40*(1), 35–41.

Chang, Y. C., Kao, M. S., Kuo, A., & Chiu, C. F. (2012). How cultural distance influences entry mode choice: The contingent role of host country's governance quality [J]. *Journal of Business Research, 65*(8), 1160–1170.

Chan, C. M., Isobe, T., & Makino, S. (2008). Which country matters? Institutional development and foreign affiliate performance [J]. *Strategic Management Journal, 29*(11), 1179–1205.

Chen, H. C., & Fan, J. H. (2013). The choice of mergers & acquisitions and green-field of chinese multinational company under the institutional distance: A study based on the angle of organizational legitimac [J]. *World Economy Studies, 12*, 53–59, 85–86.

Dacin, T. (1997). Isomorphism in context: The power and prescription of institutional norms [J]. *Academy of Management Journal, 40*(1), 46–81.

Davis, L., & North, D. (1971). *Institutional change and American economic growth*. Cambridge University Press.

Delios, A., & Henisz, W. J. (2000). Japanese firms' investment strategies in emerging economies [J]. *Academy of Management Journal, 43*(3), 305–323.

Doh, J. P., Rodrigues, P., Uhlenbruck, K., Collins, J., Eden, L., & Shekshnia, S. (2003). Coping with corruption in foreign markets. *Academy Management Executive, 17*(3), 114–127.

Dunning, J. H. (1988). The eclectic paradigm of international production: A restatement and some possible extensions [J]. *Journal of International Business Studies, 19*(1), 1–31.

Eden, L., & Miller, S. R. (2004). Distance matters: Liability of foreignness, institutional distance and ownership strategy [A]. In M. Hitt & J. Cheng (Eds.), *Advances in international management: Theories of the multinational enterprise* (Vol. 16, pp. 187–221).

Erramilli, M. K., & Rao, C. P. (1993). Service firms' international entry-mode choice: A modified transaction-cost analysis approach [J]. *The Journal of Marketing, 57*(3), 19–38.

Fagre, N., & Wells, J. L. T. (1982). Bargaining power of multinations and host governments [J]. *Journal of International Business Studies*, 9–23.

Fisher, D. O., Johnson, C. N., Lawes, M. J., Fritz, S. A., & Kutt, A. (2014). The current decline of tropical marsupials in Australia: Is history repeating? [J]. *Global Ecology and Biogeography, 23*, 181–190.

Ghemawat, P. (2001). Distance still matters [J]. *Harvard Business Review, 79*, 137–147.

Grewal, R., & Dharwadkar, R. (2002). The roal of the institutional evironment in marketing channels. *Journal of Marketing, 66*(3), 82–98.

Grosse, R., & Trevino, L. J. (1996). Foreign direct investment in the United States: An analysis by country of origin [J]. *Journal of International Business Studies, 27*(1), 139–155.

Grote, M. H., & Rucker, F. (2007). *Acquiring foreign firm far away might be hazardous to your share price: Evidence from Germany*. Goethe University, Department Finance Working Paper Series: Finance Accounting 182, Frankfurt am Main.

Habib, M., & Zurawicki, L. (2002). Corruption and foreign direct investment [J]. *Journal of International Business Studies, 33*(2), 291–307.

Hernandez, V., & Nieto, M. J. (2015). The effect of the magnitude and direction of institutional distance on the choice of international entry modes. *Journal of World Business, 50*, 122–132.

Hofstede, G. (1980). Culture and organizations [J]. *International Studies of Management & Organization, 10*(4), 15–41.

Hofstede, G., & Bond, M. H. (1988). The confucius connection: From cultural roots to economic growth. *Organizational Dynamics, 16*, 4–22.

Ionascu, D., Meyer, K., & Estrin, S. (2004). *Institutional distance and international business strategies in emerging economies* [R]. Working Paper.

Jia, J. Y., Li, W., & Guo, B. (2005). Influence of prior experience on Chinese firms' cross-border acquisitions: A study from perspective of geographic distance and government's role [J]. *Journal of International Trade, 10,* 87–97.

Johanson, J., & Vahlne, J. E. (2009). The internationalisation process of the firm: A model of knowledge development and increasing foreign market commitments [J]. *Journal of International Business Studies, 8*(1), 23–32.

Johanson, J., & Wiedersheim-Paul, F. (1975). The internationalisation of the firm: Four Swedish cases [J]. *Journal of Management Studies, 12*(3), 305–322.

Jia, P. (2008). *A study on factors influencing the OFDI entry mode choice of chinese enterprises [D]*. Central South University.

Kaufmann, D., Kraay, A., & Mastruzzi, M. (2009). *Governance matters VIII: Aggregate and individual governance indicators, 1996–2008* [R]. World Bank Policy Research Working Papers.

Kaufmann, D., Kraay, A., & Mastruzzi, M. (2010). *The worldwide governance indicators: Methodology and analytical issues* (World Bank Policy Research Working Paper No. 5430).

Kirkman, B. L., Lowe, K. B., & Gibson, C. B. (2006). A quarter century of culture's consequences: A review of empirical research incorporating Hofstede's cultural values framework [J]. *Journal of International Business Studies, 37,* 285–320.

Kogut, B., & Singh, H. (1988). The effect of national culture on the choice of entry mode [J]. *Journal of International Business Studies, 19*(3), 411–432.

Kostova, T. (1996). *Success of the multinational transfer of organisational practices within multinational companies [D]* (pp. 9–21). The University of Minnesota.

Kostova, T. (1999). Multinational transfer of strategic organisational practices: A contextual perspective [J]. *Academy of Management Review, 24,* 308–324.

Kostova, T., & Roth, K. (2002). Adoption of an organisational practice by subsidiaries of multinational corporations: Institutional and relational effects [J]. *Academy of Management Journal, 45,* 215–233.

Kostova, T., Roth, K., & Dacin, M. T. (2008). Institutional theory in the study of multinational corporations: A critique and new directions [J]. *Academy of Management Review, 33*(4), 994–1006.

Kostova, T., & Zaheer, S. (1999). Organisational legitimacy under conditions of complexity: The case of the multinational enterprise [J]. *Academy of Management Review, 24*(1), 64–81.

Lecraw, D. J. (1984). Bargaining power, ownership and the profitability of transnational corporations [J]. *Journal of International Business Studies, 15*(1), 27–43.

Li, J., & Guisinger, S. (1992). The globalization of service multinationals in the 'Triad' regions: Japan, Western Europe and North American [J]. *Journal of International Business Studies, 23*(4), 675–696.

Lopez-Duarte, C., Vidal-Suarez, M., & Gonzalez-Diaz, B. (2016). International business and national culture: A literature review and research agenda [J]. *International Journal of Management Reviews, 18*, 397–416.

Lorre, D. W., & Guisinger, S. E. (1995). Policy and non-policy determinants of U.S. equity foreign direct investment [J]. *Journal of International Business Studies, 26*(2): 281–299.

Luo, Z. (2009). The determinants of FDI inflow to China: The empirical research based on international panel data [J]. *South China Journal of Economics, 2009*(1), 33–41.

Luo, Y., & Tung, R. L. (2007). International expansion of emerging market enterprises: A springboard perspective [J]. *Journal of International Business Studies, 38*(4), 481–498.

Meyer, K. E. (2001). Institutions, transaction costs, and entry mode choice in Eastern Europe [J]. *Journal of International Business Studies, 32*(2), 357–367.

Meyer, K. E., & Peng, M. W. (2005). Probing theoretically into Central and Eastern Europe: Transactions, resources, and institutions [J]. *Journal of International Business Studies, 36*(6), 600–621.

Meyer, J. W., & Rowan, B. (1977). Institutionalized organizations: Formal structure as myth and ceremony [J]. *American Journal of Sociology*, 340–363.

Meyer, K. E., Mudambi, R., & Narula, R. (2011). Multinational enterprises and local contexts: The opportunities and challenges of multiple embeddedness [J]. *Journal of Management Studies, 48*(2), 235–252.

Meyer, K. E., Wright, M., & Pruthi, S. (2009). Research notes and commentaries managing knowledge in foreign entry strategies: A resource-based analysis [J]. *Strategic Management Journal, 30*(6), 557–574.

North, D. (1990). *Institutions, institutional change, and economic performance* [M]. Cambridge University Press.

Peng, M. W. (2003). Institutional transitions and strategic choices [J]. *Academy of Management Review, 28*(2), 275–296.

Polesello, D., Amal, M., & Hoeltgebaum, M. (2013). Determinants of international entry mode choice: A case study of a Brazilian multinational [J]. *Base, 102*(7), 181–194.

Ragozzino, R., & Reuer, J. J. (2009). Contingent earnouts in acquisitions of privately held targets [J]. *Journal of Management, 35*, 857–879.

Rodriguez, P., Uhlenbruck, K., & Eden, L. (2005). Government corruption and the entry strategies of multinationals. *Academy of Management Review, 30*(2), 383–396.

Scott, W. R. (1995). *Institutions and organisations* [M]. Sage.

Shenkar, O., Luo, Y., & Yeheskel, O. (2008). From "distance" to "friction": Substituting metaphors and redirecting intercultural research [J]. *Academy of Management Review, 33*, 905–923.

Shleifer, A., & Robert, V. (1993). Corruption [J]. *Quarterly Journal of Economics*, 599–617. *Journal of International Marketing, 14*(1), 49–70.

Sousa, C. M. P., & Bradley, F. (2006). Cultural distance and psychic distance: Two peas in a pod [J]. *Journal of International Marketing, 14*(1), 49–70.

Tan, J. (2009). Institutional structure and firm social performance in transitional economies: Evidence of multinational corporations in China [J]. *Journal of Business Ethics, 86*(S2), 171–189.

Thomas, D. E., & Grosse, R. (2001). Country of origin determinants of foreign direct investment in an emerging market: The case of Mexico [J]. *Journal of International Management, 7*(1), 59–79.

Van Hoorn, A. A. J., & Maseland, R. (2016). How institutions matter for international business: Institutional distance effects vs institutional profile effects [J]. *Journal of International Business Studies, 47*, 374–381.

Veugelers, R. (1991). Locational determinants and rankings of host countries. *Kyklos, 44*(3), 363–382.

Xu, D., & Shenkar, O. (2002). Note: Institutional distance and the multinational enterprise [J]. *Academy of Management Review, 27*(4), 608–618.

Yin, Z. M., Yuan, Z. B., & Fu, Z. (2013). The influence of cultural distance on multinational enterprise performance [J]. *Contemporary Economic Research, 2*, 37–41.

Zaheer, S. (1995). Overcoming the liability of foreignness [J]. *Academy of Management Journal, 38*(2), 341–363.

CHAPTER 7

The Institutional Gap and Chinese MNEs Governance

The institutional gap is a key concept in international business research (Berry et al., 2010). Recent studies have shown that despite the increasing frequency of social, cultural, and commercial exchanges between countries, there has been no decrease in the institutional distance between them (Van Hoorn & Maseland, 2016). MNEs need to constantly find a balance between the institutional demands of their home and host countries. The institutional gap remains a challenge in business internationalisation (Fortwengel, 2017).

7.1 THE INSTITUTIONAL GAP

This section expounds on the conceptual role and connotations of the institutional gap to help readers better understand how institutional distance affects the overseas investment of Chinese enterprises.

7.1.1 Conceptual Role of the Institutional Gap

Institutional distance has been a research focus since Kostova and Zaheer (1999) put forward the concept. In extending the concept of institution, Scott (2001) defined institutional distance as the differences between countries in their regulatory, normative, and cognitive institutions.

As an increasing number of enterprises from emerging economies globalise, there is increasing diversity in investment destinations. Enterprises invest in countries with well-functioning institutions but also in countries with institutional deficiencies. Therefore, the challenges associated with institutional differences arise not only from the magnitude of the institutional distance but also from the difference in the degree of institutionalisation, which is not reflected in the existing concept of institutional distance. The overly narrow definition of institutional distance has become outdated, thus undermining the applicability and explanatory power of the concept. Further research shows that, like economic distance, institutional distance concerns not only the difference in degree but also the difference in quality. The concept of the institutional gap put forward in this chapter reflects this observation of differences in degree and quality between the regulatory institutions of different countries.

7.1.2 Connotations of the Institutional Gap

7.1.2.1 A Dichotomous View of Institutional Distance

North (1990) defined institutions as a series of constraints designed to regulate people's behaviour in their political, economic, and social interactions, thus defining the rules of the game in society. According to North, institutions can be divided into formal rules and informal constraints. Formal rules are those that economic participants must abide by, such as political rules and legal decisions, represented by the constitution, laws, and property rights. Informal constraints refer to the restrictions naturally derived from people's interactions and embody the beliefs, norms, and values shared by the members of society, such as taboos, traditions, and codes of conduct. Following North's division of institutions, a large body of research has defined the institutional distance between countries as the difference between their formal and informal institutions, and the meanings of the two institutions have continued to evolve.

In 1991, Gray interpreted formal institutions as comprising three dimensions: (1) the development of rules and standards according to laws and regulations, (2) law enforcement, and (3) dispute mediation. Formal institutions mostly take the form of legal documents, which are relatively transparent and readily accessible to enterprises. Formal institutional distance refers to the difference between countries in the above three dimensions. Whitley's (1999) definition of informal institution proposed that informal institutions are culture-based and related to actors' attitudes to trust, cooperation, identity, and subordination. Informal institutions are regarded as the codes of conduct of actors embedded in specific cultures and ideologies. A country's institutions are designed to reduce the uncertainties in society and create an orderly social environment. Some studies have suggested that organisations are subject not only to formal and informal institutions external to the organisation but also to internal formal and informal rules, which play an important role in an enterprise's endeavour to gain and maintain a competitive edge. Institutional distance has also been divided into formal and informal types, with empirical studies having verified each MNEs' entry strategies (Chan et al., 2008; Peng, 2003; Qi & Zou, 2013).

The dichotomous view distinguishes between the formal and informal institutions of a country. Based on the connotations of formal and informal institutions, it is evident that the formal institutions of different countries vary in quality. However, there is no such judgement of quality to be made in regard to informal institutions, which only reflect the distinctive features of a country or region. On a dichotomous basis, therefore, the institutional gap is the sum of a formal institutional surplus or deficit and an informal institutional gap.

7.1.2.2 A Trichotomous View of Institutional Distance

Kostova (1996) put forward the concept of institutional distance based on North's definition of the institution. Since then, institutional distance has been a focus of academic interest. Kostova initially hypothesised that institutional distance is the extent of dissimilarity between the normative, cognitive, and regulatory institutions of two countries. Scott (2001) extended the concept of the institution by putting forward a theoretical framework consisting of three dimensions of institutions (regulatory, normative, and cognitive). He defined institutional distance as the differences between countries in their regulatory, normative, and cognitive systems and believed that these systems would affect the behaviour of organisations and individuals. Xu and Shenkar (2002) also defined institutional distance as the regulatory, normative, and cognitive distance between countries. Regulatory distance refers to the difference in laws and regulations between countries, normative distance refers to the difference in social norms between countries, and cognitive distance refers to the difference in beliefs and values between countries. In many empirical studies, cognitive distance has been regarded as cultural distance.

The three dimensions of institutions (regulatory, normative, and cognitive) endow organisations with three kinds of legitimacy. The regulatory dimension emphasises organisations' compliance with rules and regulations for the purpose of gaining legitimacy and is concerned with pressure from formal regulatory procedures, which formulate rules, supervise the activity, and punish deviance. An organisation fully complying with these rules and regulations is deemed legal by stakeholders. The normative dimension stresses the role of the administrative system. Organisations are not only bound by general social norms, such as the norm of fair competition, but also by professional standards recognised by practitioners. Compared with the regulatory dimension, the normative dimension is more likely to be internalised by organisations. The cognitive dimension mainly concerns being understood and recognised. Legitimacy on this dimension can be obtained by observing the recognised definitions and system of references within the shared context of an organisation's operations.

According to the trichotomous view of institutions, regulatory institutions vary in quality across different countries, but no judgement of quality can be made regarding normative and cognitive institutions, which are measured only by their divergence. Therefore, the institutional gap is divided into a regulatory, institutional surplus and deficit, normative institutional gap, and cognitive institutional gap on a trichotomous basis.

7.2 Institutional Gap and MNEs Governance

This section investigates the literature mainly from the perspective of institutional surplus and institutional deficit to provide an overview of the multinational investment patterns of certain countries.

7.2.1 *Institutional Deficit and MNEs Governance*

7.2.1.1 *Location Selection for OFDI*

Some scholars have found an imbalanced geographical distribution of Chinese OFDI stock and overseas branches (Wang, 2003). For example, UNCTAD Handbook of statistics (2005) pointed out that from 1979 to 2002, about 62% of Chinese OFDI went to Hong Kong, the US, Canada, and Australia. However, few empirical studies have been on the influence of host country factors on the location selection for Chinese

OFDI. Buckley et al. (2007) established a model to validate the influence of host country factors on the location of Chinese OFDI using data from the 1984 to 2001 period. Some Chinese scholars, such as Zhang et al. (2007) and Wen (2008), have also discussed the decisive role of host country characteristics in Chinese OFDI. However, most empirical studies of the influence of host country factors on the location selection for Chinese OFDI have focused on the effects of particular non-institutional factors (Wen, 2008; Zhang et al., 2007), with only a few including institutional variables such as political risk, foreign investment openness, and host country language and culture (Buckley et al., 2007; Wen, 2008).

7.2.1.2 Host Country Selection

Some studies have classified host country markets based on the quality of their institutions. These studies suggest that enterprises should invest in developed countries with sound institutions because they can provide better protection for foreign enterprises and help them avoid many operational risks. One study found a positive relationship between the quality of legal institutions of developing countries and Chinese OFDI, but the legal institutions of developed countries had no significant effect (Deng, 2012). Jiang and Jiang (2012) pointed out that Chinese OFDI tends to flow to host countries with better supervision quality, higher government efficiency, and better legal and corruption control than China.

Qi and Zou (2013) incorporated the dichotomy between formal and informal institutions into their study on host country selection, holding that host countries with higher-quality formal institutions (economic institutions and legal institutions) would attract more overseas investment in general, but that higher informal institutional distance (cultural distance) would hinder Chinese enterprises from investing in the host country.

7.2.1.3 Choice of Equity Entry Mode

Some studies on the entry mode of MNEs from the perspective of formal institutions have focused on the risks to enterprises associated with the formal institutions of host countries. However, a sound institutional system is beneficial to business activities (Gelbuda et al., 2008), and some studies have detected a positive correlation between formal institutions and entry mode (Kwon & Konopa, 1993). For example, Wu (2011) investigated the overseas investment behaviour of Chinese enterprises through a questionnaire survey. Although there were only 243 valid responses out of 865 questionnaires distributed, the results suggest that the higher the quality of formal institutions in a host country, the more likely Chinese enterprises enter the local market through M&As and establish wholly-owned companies.

7.2.2 Institutional Surplus and MNEs Governance

7.2.2.1 Location Selection for OFDI

In their analysis of the influence of the host country's institutional quality on the location choice for Chinese OFDI, Zhang and Wang (2009) found that higher institutional quality encouraged inflows of Chinese OFDI. It is generally believed that a high level of corruption—a marker of poor-quality institutions—is a 'grabbing hand' of FDI because it increases bribery and rent-seeking costs and adds to the uncertainties involved in contract execution. However, corruption may also act as a 'helping hand' if MNEs are willing to pay bribes to avoid bureaucratic inefficiencies or more easily gain access to projects financed by public funds in the host country. When the benefit of this 'helping hand' exceeds the cost of the 'grabbing hand', the poor institutional quality represented by corruption promotes FDI inflows (Egger & Winner, 2005).

7.2.2.2 Host Country Selection

The first step of internationalisation is to select a target market, which is a primary determinant for the eventual outcome of an MNE's internationalisation strategy (Andersen & Strandskov, 1998; Melin, 1992). The choice of the target market (i.e. host country) is a key issue in enterprise internationalisation and has received significant academic attention. The topic has been explored from a diverse range of perspectives.

One approach has been to divide enterprises into those in developed countries and those in developing countries. As enterprise internationalisation progresses, increasing numbers of enterprises invest in countries or regions with different institutions from their home countries, as in the case of enterprises from developed countries investing in developing countries (Bevan & Estrin, 2004; Dikova & Witteloostuijn, 2007; Hoskisson et al., 2000). Developing countries differ significantly from developed countries in their institutional frameworks, and most enterprises in developing countries are state-owned. Consequently, state ownership affects enterprise behaviour to a certain extent. Although the governments of many developing countries have pushed for the privatisation of state-owned companies, they remain actively involved in the operations of enterprises studies. Therefore, enterprises from developed countries should learn to deal with local governments properly when choosing to operate in developing countries (Meyer et al., 2009; Ramamurti, 2000; Uhlenbruck et al., 2006).

Some scholars argue that enterprises should give priority to investing in underdeveloped areas to seize more markets and resources. For example, Tang (2012) studied the entry mode choice of large-scale construction enterprises entering the African market and argued that Chinese enterprises should first choose underdeveloped countries or regions to quickly occupy the market before business expansion.

7.2.2.3 Choice of Equity Entry Mode

According to some studies, weak formal institutions impede transactions (Peng & Luo, 2000). For example, if the host country does not provide property protection, foreign enterprises are exposed to significant risks in transactions, which hinder their local trading activities. Therefore, there is a positive correlation between formal institutions and the entry mode (Brouthers & Nakos, 2004).

7.2.3 Institutional Similarity and MNEs Governance

Another strand of the literature proceeds from the perspective of institutional similarity between the host and home countries. For M&As, Yan et al. (2009) found that less cultural distance was associated with better performance, suggesting that Chinese MNEs should invest in culturally similar countries to China. Wang (2005) probed different stages of internationalisation and posited that in the initial stage, international retailers prefer host countries with cultural, psychological, and market proximity to their home countries, and Johanson and Vahlne (2009) studied several Swedish MNEs and found that they chose Denmark, Norway, and Finland, which are at a short psychic distance from Sweden, as host countries. Other studies have come to the same conclusion that MNEs are more willing to invest in host countries with similar institutions because this provides less uncertainty in their operations (Habib & Zurawicki, 2002). For example, Buckley et al. (2007) found that Chinese enterprises, most of which were state-owned, tended to invest in countries with similar politics and institutions. Claessens and Van Horen (2008) corroborated this finding through an empirical study of the banking industry in 'Southern Cone' countries. They posited that familiarity with the host country's institutional environment could reduce the operating costs of MNEs and make it easier to fit into the local business environment.

In reviewing the literature, we found that although many scholars have noticed the influences of different levels of institutional quality on MNEs' governance, none have explicated a general law for these effects. Therefore, the third section of this chapter focuses on how institutional difference—captured in the concept of the institutional gap—affects the governance of Chinese MNEs.

7.3 The Institutional Gap and the Governance of Equity Ownership in Foreign Subsidiaries of Chinese MNEs

Based on the literature, this section analyses how institutional surplus and institutional deficit affect the governance of Chinese MNEs by drawing on transaction cost theory and institutional theory.

7.3.1 Formal Institution Deficit and the Governance of Equity Ownership in Foreign Subsidiaries of Chinese MNEs

As described above, formal institutions are mainly reflected in the laws and regulations, law enforcement efficiency, and dispute mediation. Many studies have shown that enterprises have better operating results in countries with higher institutional quality (Globerman & Shapiro, 2003), encouraging them to invest in these countries to avoid the restrictions imposed by unfavourable institutions in their own countries (Luo & Tung, 2007). Countries with a higher level of institutional quality provide a well-established institutional system with greater fairness, transparency, and stability, more advanced public infrastructure, and a relatively free and open business environment. Higher formal institutional quality equates to well-developed laws and regulations. Enterprises operating in such an institutional environment can more easily access information on the rules and regulations they must follow and enjoy more advanced public infrastructure and a relatively free and open business environment. Moreover, in a sound institutional system, laws and regulations are formulated and implemented formally, making it easier for enterprises to gain legitimacy through regulatory compliance. Studies have shown that once MNEs obtain institutional legitimacy and the resources needed for development in the host country and acquaint themselves with the local situation, legitimacy acquisition ceases to be their focus (Chang & Rosenzweig, 2001; Li & Meyer, 2009). The most relevant factor affecting operations in the host country is the coordination between the parent and subsidiary companies, such as information exchange and internal knowledge transfer.

After setting up subsidiaries in the new market, parent companies are primarily concerned with the performance of subsidiaries and managing the exchange of information between them, such as the transfer of their exclusive competitive edges to overseas subsidiaries (Dunning, 1995). Jia (2008) showed that high equity ownership in subsidiaries facilitates the transfer of knowledge, experience, and core competitiveness between parent companies and subsidiaries and gives a greater level of control to parent companies, which improves their management efficiency. In addition, enterprises can benefit more from an external environment with a better-developed institutional system (Chan et al., 2008).

In summary, when entering a country with a sound institutional system (i.e. the home market has an institutional deficit), MNEs pay more attention to the flow of knowledge between parent and subsidiary companies. When there is a great difference in formal institutions between the home and host countries, enterprises tend to establish wholly-owned subsidiaries to maintain internal consistency between the parent and subsidiary companies. In other words, in situations of institutional deficit, the greater the difference in formal institutions, the more likely enterprises are to set up wholly-owned subsidiaries.

7.3.2 *Formal Institutional Surplus and the Governance of Equity Ownership in Foreign Subsidiaries of Chinese MNEs*

Countries with weaker formal institutions can possess competitive advantages in the cost of labour and natural resources (Dunning, 1998), which is a significant factor in attracting foreign investment. However, these countries generally have unsound legal systems featuring ambiguous definitions and boundaries, which present a major obstacle to enterprises' operations and technology transfer in particular (Coeurderoy & Murray, 2008), which hinder the product innovation of MNEs operating in these countries (Wu, 2013). Moreover, weaker formal institutions can be associated with more severe corruption due to a lack of supervision, thus impeding the inflow of foreign capital (Javorcik & Wei, 2009) and increasing operating risks. It has been shown that when an MNE enters a country with an unsound institutional environment, it focuses more on internal consistency than legitimacy acquisition (Yiu & Makino, 2002). MNEs often find it hard to observe local laws and regulations in countries with weaker formal institutions and thus find it more difficult to gain local legitimacy (Håkanson & Ambos, 2010; Schwens et al., 2011). The lower the quality of formal institutions, the more difficult it is for MNEs to gain legitimacy locally, and the higher the operational risk and uncertainty are.

To sum up, when investing in countries with poor-quality formal institutions, MNEs pay more attention to the acquisition of external legitimacy than to internal consistency. Under these circumstances, they are more likely to establish subsidiaries through joint ventures with local partners (Agarwal & Ramaswami, 1992) to fit into the local market and gain local legitimacy. In contrast, when investing in countries with high-quality formal institutions, MNEs are more inclined to establish wholly-owned subsidiaries due to the formal institutional difference between the home and host countries. Therefore, when in a situation of institutional surplus, the greater the difference in formal institutions, the more likely are enterprises to set up wholly-owned subsidiaries.

7.3.3 *Informal Institutional Differences and the Governance of Equity Ownership in Foreign Subsidiaries of Chinese MNEs*

Compared with formal institutions, informal institutions operate more implicitly and are thus more difficult to discern and grasp (Beamish, 1985). Setting up joint ventures in a context of great informal institutional differences between the home and the countries makes it difficult for MNEs to understand their local partners, which increases the possibility of speculative behaviour on the part of the partners. To reduce the damage to corporate interests caused by speculative behaviour, MNEs need to supervise the partnership and partners' behaviour more closely, which incur additional costs (Chang et al., 2012).

When operating subsidiaries in foreign markets, MNEs need to consider how to transfer the core competitiveness, such as management experience, from the parent company to the subsidiaries. For joint ventures, conflicts in operations and management between the two sides and communication issues between employees from the two countries are inevitable. Greater informal institutional differences are associated with greater difficulties in communication between the parent and subsidiary companies. The informal institutional difference in this case mainly arises from different operations and management backgrounds and different paradigms and values held by employees. These differences increase the difficulty of communication between employees from the two countries (Luo, 2009), which dramatically increases the cost of knowledge transfer from parent companies to subsidiaries and thus increases the overall enterprise management costs (Anand & Delios, 1997). A high percentage of ownership makes it easier for an MNE to successfully transfer knowledge, experience, and core competitiveness to their subsidiaries. Moreover, a higher investment ratio means greater decision-making power and higher efficiency (Jia, 2008). Therefore, the greater the difference in informal institutions, the more likely enterprises are to set up wholly-owned subsidiaries.

The difference between Chinese culture and foreign cultures constitutes an informal institutional gap that can be measured using the definitions of Hofstede and the measurement model of Kogut and Singh (1988). Their research drew upon data collected for compiling the national cultural distance index from The Hofstede Centre. The four cultural dimensions are power distance, individualism/collectivism, masculinity/femininity, and uncertainty avoidance. The formula for calculating cultural distance is as follows:

$$CD_j = \sum_{i=1}^{4} \left\{ (I_{ij} - I_{iu})^2 / V_i \right\} / 4 \qquad (7.1)$$

where I_{ij} represents the score of the host country where the foreign subsidiaries of MNEs are located in the cultural dimension i, I_{iu} represents the score of the home country (China) of MNEs in the cultural dimension i, and V_i represents the variance of the cultural dimension i. In an empirical study of the relationship between Chinese culture and the governance of Chinese MNEs, Xu and Li (2011) found a strong negative correlation between cultural differences and Chinese FDI. A greater cultural difference between the host country and China was associated with less Chinese direct investment in the host country. In an empirical study on the influence of cultural distance and ethnic Chinese networks in the host country on Chinese FDI location selection based on the negative binomial regression model using panel data of enterprise-level FDI projects, Zhang and Li (2014) found that greater cultural distance between the host country and China had a significant inhibitory effect on Chinese FDI. However, the presence of ethnic Chinese networks in the host country significantly promoted Chinese FDI.

7.3.4 Host Country Institutions, the Institutional Gap, and the Governance of Equity Ownership in Foreign Subsidiaries of Chinese MNEs

When considering an overseas investment, one common issue facing MNEs is that the host country might have strict restrictions on entry modes and investment strategies, some of which might constitute barriers to entry. For example, some international business researchers have pointed out that restrictions on foreign ownership imposed by a host country might prevent MNEs from entering by establishing wholly-owned companies. Therefore, some countries reduce restrictions on foreign investment to encourage MNEs to enter the local market, especially in industries that were previously protected by the state or have high barriers to entry, to promote the development of these industries. Studies suggest that the degree of openness to foreign investment in the host country is one of the major concerns for MNEs when choosing the entry mode, with different countries having standards of different openness. Compared with developed countries, developing countries tend to rely more on government restrictions.

MNEs generally devote more resources and investment commitments to markets with good external environments. Therefore, countries with fewer restrictions on foreign investment can easily attract MNEs even in cases of major differences between the host and home countries in formal or informal institutions. However, the research on this topic has been based on enterprises in developed economies. Enterprises based in the emerging economy of China need to deal with a completely different environmental gap from that experienced by enterprises in developed economies when entering foreign markets. China is still undergoing an economic transition, and it was not long ago that Chinese enterprises made their first steps into the international market. Many are therefore unfamiliar with the business model and environment of overseas markets. As they are still moving cautiously towards internationalisation, Chinese enterprises are relatively risk-averse in foreign environments, even those that are favourable to business. A host country that is more open to foreign investment has lower entry barriers to attract enterprises from many countries. However, when there is the great institutional distance between the host country and China, Chinese enterprises have to compete with enterprises from countries that are institutionally similar to the host country. These competitors have the advantage of being familiar with the institutions in the host country, with the Chinese enterprises facing greater uncertainty and risk. In response, Chinese enterprises tend to spread the risks by partnering with local enterprises through a transfer of equity.

However, as mentioned above, formal institutions are different from informal institutions in that the former is more transparent, whereas the latter is generally embedded in social constructs. When investing in a host country with high formal institutional distance and a high level of openness to foreign investment, Chinese enterprises are at a disadvantage compared to their competitors because formal institutions are readily accessible. Therefore, the greater the difference in formal institutions, the more likely enterprises are to set up joint ventures. However, in a host country with a high level of openness to foreign investment, the environmental differences associated with informal institutional distance are less perceptible to Chinese enterprises and their competitors. Markets with high levels of openness to foreign capital also have lower entry barriers and thus attract more MNEs, including enterprises from emerging economies like China, compared with markets that are less open to foreign investment. The increase of foreign enterprises results in stricter implicit supervision of local enterprises, which may prevent the speculative behaviour of local enterprises to a certain extent. Therefore, a high level of openness to foreign investment might weaken the positive relationship between informal institutional distance and equity control. Two research questions arise from this observation: (1) When MNEs from emerging economies enter host countries with high institutional quality and a high level of openness to foreign investment, is a greater difference in formal institutions associated with a greater likelihood of enterprises setting up joint ventures? (2) When MNEs from emerging economies enter host countries with high institutional quality and a high level of openness to foreign investment, does this high level of openness to foreign investment weaken the positive relationship between informal institutional distance and equity control?

Governments can implement policy changes to ease restrictions on foreign investment and attract foreign investment (Flores & Aguilera, 2007), which promote the country's economic development (Aghion et al., 2008). As MNEs prefer to invest in countries with good external market environments (Dunning & Lundan, 2008), openness to foreign investment encourages enterprises to invest in a country. A formal institutional surplus refers to the situation in which the host country has lower institutional quality and a less sound institutional system than the home country. The stakeholders embedded in such a system are under little mandatory pressure. As the host country becomes more open, the increase in foreign investment leads to greater supervision of local enterprises by their foreign counterparts, alleviating the influence of institutional distance on enterprise decision-making. Therefore, when Chinese MNEs enter a host country with low institutional quality and a high level of openness to foreign investment, a greater formal institutional distance between the two countries is associated with a greater likelihood of enterprises maintaining high equity ownership when setting up subsidiaries. Furthermore, when Chinese MNEs enter a host country with high institutional quality and a high level of openness to foreign investment, a greater informal institutional distance between the two countries is associated with a greater likelihood of enterprises maintaining high equity ownership when setting up subsidiaries.

7.3.5 *Diversification Strategy, the Institutional Gap, and the Governance of Equity Ownership in Foreign Subsidiaries of Chinese MNEs*

According to the theory of enterprise internationalisation, MNEs adopt a diversification strategy. As the parent company establishes more overseas subsidiaries (wholly-owned or by joint venture), its percentage of ownership in foreign subsidiaries may decrease because of its limited resource endowment; however, the parent company may be able to acquire a higher ownership stake in foreign subsidiaries by fully utilising its resources and thus might still choose the wholly-owned entry mode. Wilson (1980) concluded that when enterprises with a high level of product diversification but little internationalisation experience invest in developing countries, they tend to establish foreign subsidiaries by acquisition (joint venture) rather than setting up wholly owned subsidiaries. Caves and Mehra (1986) found that the scale, product diversification, and degree of internationalisation of foreign enterprises positively and significantly affected their acquisition decisions when they entered the US manufacturing industry. Therefore, the parent company's diversification strategy can moderate the relationship between the institutional gap and the choice of equity entry mode.

Parent companies use three diversification strategies: core business diversification, related diversification, and unrelated diversification. The moderating effects of the three diversification strategies on the relationship between institutional distance and the equity entry mode of overseas subsidiaries are as follows:

(1) The moderating role of the core business diversification strategy. In an empirical study of the relationship between diversification and the choice of market entry mode in the context of FDI, Mudambi and Mudambi (2002) found that based on competitive advantages, enterprises adopting diversification are more likely to enter through M&As, whereas enterprises focusing on their core business tend to choose greenfield investment (wholly-owned). Therefore, when the host country has high institutional quality, core business-driven enterprises may choose the wholly-owned entry mode because a large institutional deficit or small institutional surplus makes it more likely that parent companies can tap into their competitive advantages; however, when the host country has a small institutional deficit or a large institutional surplus, it is harder for enterprises to leverage their core competitive advantages, so they tend to establish joint ventures. Therefore, the core business-focused strategy of parent companies has a positive moderating effect on the relationship between the institutional gap and the choice of equity entry mode.

(2) The moderating role of the related diversification strategy. The related diversification strategy is implemented when there is a correlation in production, technology, management, and marketing between an enterprise's new lines of business and its original business so that new lines of business can share the operations capabilities of the existing business. When the parent company of an MNE implements the related diversification strategy in a situation of a large institutional deficit, a wholly-owned mode of entry facilitates the transfer of the company's relevant capabilities to the new subsidiary. However, in the case of a large institutional surplus, which impedes the company's relevant capabilities from being fully leveraged due to the institutional constraints of the host country, the enterprise is more likely to establish a joint

venture to reduce operating risks. Therefore, the related diversification strategy has a positive moderating effect on the relationship between the institutional gap and the choice of equity entry mode.

(3) The moderating effect of the unrelated diversification strategy. Unrelated diversification occurs when there is no common thread between an enterprise's new and existing lines of business, such that the enterprise must gain new capabilities in such areas as production, technology, management, and marketing to avoid excessive additional costs. A large institutional deficit is more favourable for an MNE to expand unrelated business. However, the company needs to work with local enterprises to acquire unrelated resources and share relevant operating capabilities, and it is thus more likely to establish a joint venture instead of a wholly-owned subsidiary. When MNEs enter a host country with a large institutional surplus, even when the expansion of unrelated business depends greatly on cheap local labour or natural resources, the parent company may still opt for the wholly-owned equity entry mode due to high negotiating costs or because the parent company can only provide the necessary technology and management knowledge. Therefore, the unrelated diversification strategy has a negative moderating effect on the relationship between the institutional gap and the choice of equity entry mode.

7.4 THE INSTITUTIONAL GAP AND MARKET PERFORMANCE OF CHINESE OVERSEAS LISTED COMPANIES

7.4.1 Political Connections and Enterprise Value on IPO

Theoretical research into the relationship between political connections and enterprise performance has always focused on management studies. However, no consensus has been reached on this relationship. Some scholars have argued that political connections have a positive impact on enterprise performance because the political connections between entrepreneurs and government officials make it easier for enterprises to reap profits through rent-seeking. Enterprises with political connections can obtain more government procurement contracts, easier access to bank financing with more favourable loan conditions, better tax rates, more government subsidies, easier access to franchise opportunities and industry entry capabilities, more cross-regional product sales, and fewer regulatory constraints and legal sanctions.

However, some studies have noted the negative effects of political connections on corporate performance from the perspective of outside investors (Faccio, 2006; Fisman, 2001). Information asymmetry between investors and enterprise managers often causes agency problems. An agency problem may arise when the privatisation of managers' personal interests infringes on investors' interests, increasing the costs of investment and eventually reduce willingness to invest and cause a decrease in the market value of the relevant listed enterprises. For Chinese enterprises, political connections may aggravate the agency problems between investors and enterprises in four ways.

First, the senior management in most Chinese enterprises with political connections is generally appointed by the government. The blurred boundary between the government and the enterprise gives rise to agency problems. Fan et al. (2007) claimed that the Chinese government's intervention in enterprise operations by appointing government officials as CEO would damage the long-term performance of enterprises. Berkman et al. (2010) found that in China, compared with non-politically connected enterprises, the controlling shareholders of enterprises with political connections were more likely to encroach on the interests of minority shareholders. In a study on the overseas listing of Chinese SOEs, Hung et al. (2012) found that the managers of politically-connected enterprises were more likely to expand their private interests.

Second, political connections can introduce a degree of confusion to an enterprise's business motivation, which should be profit maximisation. Government officials serving as senior management in enterprises may pursue their personal political goals at the expense of the long-term profit growth of the company, in such ways as blindly expanding the scale of the enterprise, over-investing, and allocating additional resources for unproductive activities to serve the development of the local economy and increase employment. Hung et al. also found that the motivation for Chinese SOEs to go public abroad lies in political interests more than for the purpose of overseas expansion.

Third, politically connected enterprises may face more environmental uncertainties, as even slight changes in political connections can damage their operational stability. For example, the dismissal of corrupt officials often leads to negative financial performance of related public companies.

Fourth, as political connections can bring short-term benefits, such as tax incentives and bank loans, enterprises are less motivated to voluntarily disclose information to seek financing. This increases the costs of investment as investors are less likely to obtain useful information.

The above analysis shows that political connections aggravate the agency problems between enterprises and investors, making investors less willing to invest in politically connected enterprises, thus damaging corporate value. Therefore, there is a negative correlation between political connections and the corporate value of newly listed Chinese enterprises.

7.4.2 Moderating Effect of the Institutional Environment on the Relationship Between Political Connections and Enterprise Value on IPO

Institutions shape and regulate the economic activities of organisations. However, the institutional environment varies across countries and over time. Consequently, many academic studies have explored the effects of different institutional environments on the structures and processes of organisations.

The institutional environment in developed Western countries is different from that in China because their systems are organised to effectively check government power and curb corruption. These countries usually have a transparent legal system, and the contract terms and most resource allocation decisions are subject to the private sector, which contributes to stable economic development. In contrast, the weaker institutional environment in China is characterised by a concentration of decision-making power in the government, large asymmetries in market information, and ineffective social norm interventions. Moreover, the government has control over the main production resources and holds the power to intervene, but the underdeveloped laws and regulations provide inadequate protection for investors, resulting in unstable economic development. This institutional difference is also evidenced by the Index of Economic Freedom. According to the Economic Freedom of the World 2020 Annual Report, the top ten countries are Hong Kong, Singapore, New Zealand, Switzerland, Australia, the United States, Mauritius, Georgia, Canada, and Ireland. And China (mainland) ranked 124th.

The relationship between political connections and enterprise value varies in different institutional environments. Faccio (2006) found that political connections were not common in countries with strict institutions but could significantly enhance enterprise value in countries or regions with severe corruption. In the well-developed institutional environments often found in Western countries, government intervention in enterprise performance is restrained, and managers are more willing to follow the general business rules in economic activities. However, the institutional theory holds that in countries with poorly developed institutional environments, informal institutions can prevail due to the partial failure of formal institutions such as political rules and commercial laws. In China, to cope with the inadequacies in formal institutions, enterprises tend to establish political ties with the government to establish additional informal institutions for self-protection. The political connections of enterprises are social networking resources embedded in economic activities. The senior management of Chinese enterprises uses every possible means to establish their political networks to keep abreast of policy trends and maintain business advantages.

Regarding the capital market, domestic and overseas investors are also affected by the institutional environment when making investment decisions. Overseas investors in a high-level institutional environment believe that enterprises should follow general business rules. However, political connections have an influence beyond such rules. Furthermore, as political connections also aggravate agency problems, foreign investors are less willing to invest in Chinese politically connected enterprises. In contrast, domestic investors in low-quality institutional environments have mixed opinions on political connections. Some domestic investors hold a negative view of investing in politically connected enterprises out of a concern over agency problems. However, those who are deeply immersed in the Chinese institutional environment approve of political connections, regarding them as a kind of social capital that can increase an enterprise's market value. This divergence of opinion among domestic investors may weaken the negative effects of political connections on enterprise value, such that the negative relationship between political connections and enterprise value is weaker in the context of a poor-quality institutional environment.

In summary, the lower (higher) the quality of the institutional environment in which an enterprise is listed, the weaker (stronger) is the negative relationship between political connections and enterprise value. The institutional environment thus has a negative moderating effect on the relationship between political connections and the value of newly listed Chinese enterprises.

7.4.3 Comparing Investors in Foreign and Domestic Markets on Their Sensitivity to the Relationship Between Political Connections and Enterprise Value on IPO

The moderating effect of the institutional environment suggests its influence on the trends in the relationship between political connections and enterprise value, but the specific direction and strength of this relationship in both foreign and domestic markets remain unclear. We approach this issue from the perspectives of investors in domestic and foreign markets separately. In practice, due to restrictions put in place by stock trading policies, most domestic investors can only buy shares of domestically listed companies. Foreign investors have the right to buy domestic stocks, but foreign investment only accounts for a small proportion of the total investment in the domestic stock market. Thus, domestic investors and foreign investors are isolated, and their valuations of companies listed on the stock markets dominate the formation of and changes in company value.

As mentioned above, many domestic investors hold views of the political connections of Chinese listed companies that differ from those of foreign investors. Domestic investors who are immersed in the Chinese institutional environment are more likely to approve of political connections, leading to a divergence of opinion among domestic investors. In general, the negative evaluation of political connections by domestic investors is weak or even negligible.

There is a fundamental difference between domestic and foreign investors in terms of endowments. Due to their limited access to information, foreign investors face greater information asymmetry in relation to Chinese listed companies. As analysed above, foreign investors in a high-quality institutional environment uphold standardised transactions, and political connections as an indicator of insider trading increase doubt about China's standardisation of business processes. The agency problems caused by political connections further discourage foreign investment and reduce the market value of enterprises.

In summary, compared with domestic investors, among whom the negative evaluations of the political connections of Chinese listed companies may be insignificant, foreign investors have a more prominent effect on the negative relationship between political connections and market value of Chinese listed companies. Therefore, foreign investors are more sensitive to the negative relationship between political connections and the enterprise value at the initial public offering (IPO). In the domestic market, there is not a significant relationship between political connections and the enterprise value at IPO; in the foreign market, political connections are negatively correlated with the enterprise value at IPO.

In addition to clarifying that the investment environment faced by Chinese MNEs is different from that of their foreign counterparts in developed economies, the impact of an institutional surplus or deficit on the multinational governance of MNEs must also be explained. Based on the above analysis, it can be theorised that all else being equal, when Chinese MNEs invest in countries with an institutional deficit, a greater institutional distance is associated with a greater likelihood of the enterprises establishing wholly-owned subsidiaries; when the host country has an institutional surplus, a longer institutional distance is associated with a greater likelihood of the enterprises establishing joint ventures. However, the institutional characteristics of the host country and the diversification strategy of the enterprise also affect the enterprise's decision-making. In response to the concerns of academia and industry over the effects of political connections, this study has theoretically demonstrated that in the unique context of Chinese society, the effects of political connections on the enterprise value at IPO varies with different levels of institutional quality in IPO markets.

References

Agarwal, S., & Ramaswami, N. S. (1992). Choice of foreign market entry mode: Impact of ownership, location and internalisation factors. *Journal of International Business Studies, 23*(1), 1–27.

Aghion, P., Burgess, R., Redding, S., et al. (2008). The unequal effects of liberalisation: Evidence from dismantling the License Raj in India. *American Economic Review, 98*(4), 1397–1412.

Anand, J., & Delios, A. (1997). Location specificity and the transferability of downstream assets to foreign subsidiaries. *Journal of International Business Studies, 28*(3), 579–603.

Andersen, P. H., & Strandskov, J. (1998). International market selection: A cognitive mapping perspective. *Journal of Global Marketing, 11*(3), 65–84.

Beamish, P. W. (1985). The characteristics of joint ventures in developed and developing countries. *Columbia Journal of World Business, 20*(3), 13–19.

Berkman, H., Cole, R. A., & Fu, L. J. (2010). Political connections and minority-shareholder protection: Evidence from securities-market regulation in China. *Journal of Financial & Quantitative Analysis, 45*(6), 1391–1417.

Berry, H., Guillén, M. F., & Zhou, N. (2010). An institutional approach to cross-national distance. *Journal of International Business Studies, 41*(9), 1460–1480.

Bevan, A. A., & Estrin, S. (2004). The determinants of foreign direct investment into European transition economies. *Journal of Comparative Economics, 32*(4), 775–787.

Brouthers, K. D., & Nakos, G. (2004). SME entry mode choice and performance: A transaction cost perspective. *Entrepreneurship Theory and Practice, 28*(3), 229–247.

Buckley, P. J., Clegg, L. J., & Cross, A. R., et al. (2007). The determinants of Chinese outward foreign direct investment. *Journal of International Business Studies, 38*(4), 499–518.

Caves, R. E., & Mehra, S. K. (1986). Entry of foreign multinationals into the U.S. manufacturing industries. In M. E. Porter (Ed.), *Competition in Global Industries* (pp. 449–481). HBS Press.

Chan, C., Isobe, T., & Makino, S. (2008). Which country matters? Institutional development and foreign affiliate performance. *Strategic Management Journal, 29*(11), 1179–1205.

Chang, S. J., & Rosenzweig, P. M. (2001). The choice of entry mode in sequential foreign direct investment. *Strategic Management Journal, 22*(8), 747–776.

Chang, Y. C., Kao, M. S., Kuo, A., & Chiu, C. F. (2012). How cultural distance influences entry mode choice: The contingent role of host country's governance quality. *Journal of Business Research, 65*(8), 1160–1170.

Claessens, S., & Van Horen, N. (2008). *Location decisions of foreign banks and institutional competitive advantage* (DNB Working Papers, 2008).

Coeurderoy, R., & Murray, G. (2008). Regulatory environments and the location decision: Evidence from the early foreign market entries of new-technology-based firms. *Journal of International Business Studies, 39*(4), 670–687.

Deng, M. (2012). Institutional distance, "demonstration effect" and the location distribution of Chinese OFDI. *Journal of International Trade, 2*, 123–135.

Dikova, D., & Van Witteloostuijn, A. (2007). Foreign direct investment mode choice: Entry and establishment modes in transition economies. *Journal of International Business Studies, 38*(6), 1013–1033.

Dunning, J. H. (1995). Reappraising the eclectic paradigm in an age of alliance capitalism. *Journal of International Business Studies, 26*(3), 461–491.

Dunning, J. H. (1998). Location and multinational enterprise: A neglected factor. *Journal of International Business Studies, 29*(1), 45–66.

Dunning, J. H., & Lundan, S. (2008). *Multinational enterprises and the global economy* (2nd ed.). Edward Elgar.

Egger, P., & Winner, H. (2005). Evidence on corruption as an incentive for foreign direct investment. *European Journal of Political Economy, 21*(4), 932–952.

Faccio, M. (2006). Politically connected firms. *American Economic Review, 4,* 369–386.
Fan, J. P. H., Wong, T. J., & Zhang, T. (2007). Politically-connected CEOs, corporate governance and Post-IPO performance of China's newly partially privatised firms. *Journal of Financial Economics, 84*(2), 330–357.
Fisman, R. (2001). Estimating the value of political connections. *The American Economic Review, 2001*(91), 1095–1102.
Flores, R. G., & Aguilera, R. V. (2007). Globalisation and location choice: An analysis of US multinational firms in 1998 and 2000. *Journal of International Business Studies, 38*(7), 1187–1210.
Fortwengel, J. (2017). Practice transfer in organisations: The role of governance mode for internal and external fit. *Organisation Science, 28*(4), 690–710.
Gelbuda, M., Meyer, K. E., & Delios, A. (2008). International business and institutional development in Central and Eastern Europe. *Journal of International Management, 14*(1), 1–11.
Globerman, S., & Shapiro, D. (2003). Governance infrastructure and US foreign direct investment. *Journal of International Business Studies, 34*(1), 19–39.
Gray, C. (1991). Legal process and economic development: A case study of Indonesia. *World Development, 19*(7), 763–777.
Habib, M., & Zurawicki, L. (2002). Corruption and foreign direct investment. *Journal of International Business Studies, 33*(2), 291–307.
Håkanson, L., & Ambos, B. (2010). The antecedents of psychic distance. *Journal of International Management, 16*(3), 195–210.
Hoskisson, R. E., Eden, L., Lau, C. M., et al. (2000). Strategy in emerging economies. *Academy of Management Journal, 43*(3), 249–267.
Hung, M., Wong, T. J., & Zhang, T. (2012). Political considerations in the decision of Chinese SOEs to list in Hong Kong. *Journal of Accounting and Economics, 53*(1–2), 435–449.
Javorcik, B., & Wei, S. (2009). Corruption and cross-border investment in emerging markets: Firm level evidence. *Journal of International Money and Finance, 28*(4), 605–624.
Jia, P. (2008). *A study on factors influencing the OFDI entry mode choice of Chinese Enterprises.* Central South University.
Jiang, G. H., & Jiang, D. C. (2012). China's foreign investment location choice: Investment based on the gravity model of panel data. *The Journal of World Economy, 2012*(9), 21–40.
Johanson, J., & Vahlne, J. E. (2009). The internationalisation process of the firm: A model of knowledge development and increasing foreign market commitments [J]. *Journal of International Business Studies, 8*(1), 23–32.
Kogut, B., & Singh, H. (1988). The effect of national culture on the choice of entry mode. *Journal of International Business Studies, 19*(3), 411–432.

Kostova, T. (1996). *Success of the multinational transfer of organisational practices within multinational companies* (pp. 9–21). The University of Minnesota.

Kostova, T., & Zaheer, S. (1999). Organisational legitimacy under conditions of complexity: The case of the multinational enterprise [J]. *Academy of Management Review, 24*(1), 64–81.

Kwon, Y. C., & Konopa, L. J. (1993). Impact of host country market characteristics on the choice of foreign market entry mode. *International Marketing Review, 10*(2), 60–76.

Li, P. Y., & Meyer, K. E. (2009). Contextualising experience effects in international business: A study of ownership strategies. *Journal of World Business, 44*(4), 370–382.

Luo, Z. (2009). The determinants of FDI inflow to China: The empirical research based on international panel data. *South China Journal of Economics, 2009*(1), 33–41.

Luo, Y., & Tung, R. L. (2007). International expansion of emerging market enterprises: A springboard perspective. *Journal of International Business Studies, 38*(4), 481–498.

Melin, L. (1992). Internationalisation as a strategy process. *Strategic Management Journal, 13*, 99–118.

Meyer, K. E., Wright, M., & Pruthi, S. (2009). Research notes and commentaries managing knowledge in foreign entry strategies: A resource-based analysis. *Strategic Management Journal, 30*(6), 557–574.

Mudambi, R., & Mudambi, S. M. (2002). Diversification and market entry choices in the context of foreign direct investment. *International Business Review, 11*(1), 35–55.

North, D. C. (1990). *Institutions, institutional change and economic performance.* Cambridge University Press.

Peng, M. W. (2003). Institutional transitions and strategic choices. *Academy of Management Review, 28*(2), 275–296.

Peng, M. W., & Luo, Y. D. (2000). Managerial ties and firm performance in a transition economy: The nature of a micro-macro link [J]. *Academy of Management Journal, 3*(43), 486–501.

Qi, C. L., & Zou, C. (2013). Host country institutional quality, institutional distance and Chinese OFDI location. *Contemporary Finance & Economics, 7*, 100–110.

Ramamurti, R. (2000). Risks and rewards in the globalisation of telecommunications in emerging economies. *Journal of World Business, 35*(2), 149–170.

Schwens, C., Eiche, J., & Kabst, R. (2011). The moderating impact of informal institutional distance and formal institutional risk on SME entry mode choice. *Journal of Management Studies, 48*(2), 330–351.

Scott, W. R. (2001). *Institutions and organisations.* Sage Publications.

Tang, L. (2012). Choice of market entry mode for multinational operation of large construction enterprises—A case study of the African market. *Journal of International Economic Cooperation, 11*, 24–26.

Uhlenbruck, K., Rodriguez, P., Doh, J., et al. (2006). The impact of corruption on entry strategy: Evidence from telecommunication projects in emerging economies. *Organisation Science, 17*(3), 402–414.

United Nations Conference on Trade and Development (UNCTAD). (2005). UNCTAD Handbook of Statistics 2005.

Van Hoorn, A., & Maseland, R. (2016). How institutions matter for international business: Institutional distance effects vs institutional profile effects. *Journal of International Business Studies, 47*(3), 374–381.

Wang, N. (2003). *Measuring transaction costs: An incomplete survey* (Working Paper), Ronald Coase Institute. http://www.coase.org/workingpapers/wp-2.pdf

Wang, X. H. (2005). Mechanism of overseas market selection of international retailers—A explanation from market proximity model and psychic distance. *China Industrial Economics, 7*, 119–126.

Wen, K. L. (2008). Empirical study on determinants of Chinese OFDI—Based on the characteristics of host country. *World Economic Outlook, 10*, 18–23.

Whitley, R. (1999). *Divergent capitalisms: The social structuring and change of business systems.* Oxford University Press.

Wilson, B. D. (1980). The propensity of multinational firms to expand through acquisitions. *Journal of International Business Studies, 11*, 59–65.

Wu, J. (2013). Diverse institutional environments and product innovation of emerging market firms. *Management International Review, 53*(1), 39–59.

Wu, X. M. (2011). Institutional environment and OFDI entry modes of Chinese enterprises. *Economic Management Journal, 33*(4), 68–79.

Xu, H. L., & Li, L. H. (2011). Cultural differences impact on China's foreign direct investment location choice analysis. *Statistics & Decision, 17*, 154–156.

Xu, D., & Shenkar, O. (2002). Institutional distance and the multinational enterprise. *Academy of Management Review, 27*(4), 608–618.

Yan, D. Y., Hong, J. J., & Ren, B. (2009). The determinants of outward direct investment by chinese enterprises: An empirical study from institutional perspective [J]. *Nankai Business Review, 12*(06), 135–142, 149.

Yiu, D., & Makino, S. (2002). The choice between joint venture and wholly owned subsidiary: An institutional perspective. *Organisation Science, 13*, 667–683.

Zhang, J. P., & Li, N. (2014). Cultural distance, the overseas Chinese network with the Chinese enterprise foreign direct investment location choice. *Special Zone Economy, 1*, 93–95.

Zhang, H., & Wang, J. (2009). An empirical investigation on locational factors and China's OFDI: Based on quantile regression. *China Industrial Economics, 6*, 151–160.

Zhang, X. L., Wang, W. M., & Wang, C. (2007). An empirical research on the determinants of China's foreign direct investment. *Journal of International Trade, 5*, 91–95.

CHAPTER 8

Governance Structure and Mechanism of Chinese MNEs

The literature has provided theoretical analyses and descriptions of behavioural patterns in the governance practices of Chinese MNEs. Drawing on these findings, this chapter summarises the differences in governance structure and mechanism between Chinese MNEs and those established in developed economies to help readers understand the theoretical framework of Chinese MNEs' governance.

8.1 GOVERNANCE STRUCTURE OF CHINESE MNEs

Centred on the board of directors, this chapter analyses the unique governance structure of Chinese MNEs from the perspectives of shareholders, directors, managers, and stakeholders.

8.1.1 *Rights and Interests of Controlling Shareholders and Minority Shareholders*

An unbalanced distribution of interests between majority shareholders and minority shareholders of enterprises in emerging markets may lead to agent–agent conflicts. Diverging from the research into traditional principal-agent problems from the perspective of a conflict of interests between managers and shareholders, we focus on the conflict between two agents: majority shareholders and minority shareholders. Generally, majority shareholders focus on profit maximisation and long-term business growth, whereas minor shareholders are more concerned with short-term benefits, such as stock price appreciation and dividends. This conflict offers a new perspective on the governance of Chinese MNEs. The agent–agent conflict arises because minority shareholders do not participate in the company's decision-making processes, so there is a high possibility that majority shareholders infringe on the interests of minority shareholders.

International investors' expectations of the multinational business information of listed companies in emerging markets may affect the market value of the companies. Chen and Young (2010) pointed out that international investors tend to react to the announcement of M&As of listed companies in emerging markets. Ning et al. (2014) studied how international investors react to the announcement of cross-border M&As of listed companies in emerging markets when facing different types of majority shareholders. From a study of Chinese MNEs listed in Hong Kong from 1991 to 2010, Ning et al. found that international investors reacted positively (as reflected in an increase in the stock price) to the presence of large shareholders but negatively to the presence of institutional shareholders. Having the largest shareholder as either the state or the corporate founder has a negative impact on the stock price because international investors believe that such a governance structure may cause agent–agent conflicts. The size and independence of the board of directors have positive effects on the stock price, but an oversized board of supervisors leads to negative reactions.

A high degree of ownership concentration can also give rise to agent–agent conflicts. Ownership concentration manifests as a high shareholding ratio of large shareholders, which implies that corporate control is highly concentrated in the hands of a small number of large shareholders who dominate the company's decision-making process. Research suggests that when the degree of ownership concentration is low, controlling shareholders can focus more on the performance growth of enterprises. In contrast, a high degree of ownership concentration leads controlling shareholders to pursue their interests at the expense of the interests of minority shareholders (Lu et al., 2009). Hu and Cui (2014) examined the identity of the actual controller, the role of non-controlling shareholders' ownership, and their interaction with CEOs' rights by integrating the resource-based view and the principal-agent theory. Using a sample of 224 Chinese listed companies, they found that domestic institutional investors and the ownership of overseas companies were positively correlated with OFDI preference. However, CEOs' rights had a moderating effect on this relationship. The study revealed the effects of key governance factors (the form of ownership of various shareholders), individually and collectively, on the OFDI preferences of emerging enterprises.

Most Chinese MNEs are state-held companies. The impact of this governance model on FDI has been a particular focus of research into the governance of Chinese MNEs. The study published by Morck et al. (2008) in the *Journal of International Business Studies* found that Chinese OFDI was mostly state-controlled. The data show that Chinese MNEs, most of which were SOEs with monopoly power, tended to invest in tax havens and Southeast Asian countries in the initial stage of OFDI. The empirical analysis found that China's deposit rate, the structure of corporate property rights, and the allocation of bank-controlled capital were positively correlated with the radical growth of Chinese OFDI. In terms of investment behaviour, most active participants were motivated to over-invest, but under capital pressure, the enterprises lost other value investing opportunities. Another case study on the cross-border M&As of Chinese enterprises explored whether having the government as the largest shareholder could damage the interests of minority shareholders (Chen & Young, 2010). According to the findings, cross-border M&As in which the government is the acquirer's major shareholder may result in abnormal market value performance. Therefore, small and medium-sized investors have reason to worry about the impact of cross-border M&As on the performance of government-controlled enterprises, which is reflected in abnormal fluctuations in stock prices.

8.1.2 Board of Directors

A multinational activity represents the outcome of major business decisions of a company, which need to be approved by the board of directors before being implemented. Therefore, the characteristics of the board of directors could affect the outcomes of multinational activity. To examine how the management decisions of the board of directors affect multinational actions, Xie and Lyn (2009) studied how private enterprises and small and medium-sized MNEs in China made management decisions during multinational operations. The study also probed the role of social networks in strategy formulation and decision-making on competition and marketing. The analysis of interview data indicated that cultural and ethnic factors were key to the success of the multinational activity. Lu et al. (2009), using a sample of Chinese listed companies, concluded that having outside directors and CEOs holding shares helps enterprises make foreign trade decisions, and ownership concentration has a non-monotonic effect on this correlation. Some studies have also discussed the effects of different decision-making styles of the board on the entry mode of foreign investment. For example, Ji and Dimitratos (2013) examined the influence of rational decision-making and hierarchical concentration on decision-making effectiveness (DME) regarding international entry mode. Their study was the first to analyse the DME of international entry mode decisions based on behavioural processes from the perspective of strategic decision-making processes. A study of 233 international private companies in China showed that rational decision-making had a positive impact on DME, hierarchical concentration had a negative impact on DME, and environmental uncertainty had a negative moderating effect on rational decision-making and hierarchical concentration.

8.1.3 Managers and Executive Pay

International business decisions are implemented by management. Research on Chinese MNE governance has examined manager-related issues from two perspectives: first, the characteristics of managers themselves and the principal-agent relationship between managers and shareholders, and second, the influence of executive pay on enterprise performance.

In terms of manager characteristics, Chinese managers demonstrate greater reliance on their original social networks and a lack of international experience in internationalisation, leading to a series of multinational governance problems. Peng and Luo (2000) held that managers' social relations and social networks influence enterprises' strategic decisions and performance, suggesting a relationship between managers' connections at the micro-level and enterprise performance at the macro-level. In Western developed economies, with relatively stable economic and social structures, managers can follow the economic rules of other enterprises in the same industry in their business operations. Frequent interaction with local enterprises is conducive to understanding the overall institutional environment (Peng, 1997). In China, most managers are willing to cultivate complicated and extensive interpersonal relationships that shape their business and social activities. Chua et al. (2009) compared the configurations of the trust relationships of Chinese and American managers in their professional networks. An egocentric network was prevalent among Chinese managers, and affect- and cognition-based trust were more intertwined for Chinese than for American managers. The effect of economic exchange on affect-based trust was more prominent for Chinese managers than American ones, whereas the effect of friendship was more positive for American managers. The connections-based social network of Chinese managers only works in China and is not as helpful as expected in cross-border M&As. Cross-border M&As involve a great deal of information exchange between the acquirer and the acquiree. However, it is difficult for Chinese acquirers to reach a consensus on the key business with the acquirees, which results in higher coordination costs for each merger and acquisition transaction and can even cause deals to fail (Peng & Luo, 2000).

Managers' levels of international experience play a key role in multinational business expansion. Studies have explored how Chinese enterprises can acquire multinational governance experience and successfully expand business overseas, mostly from the perspective of organisational learning. Building on an organisational learning perspective, Rabbiosi et al. (2012) posited that emerging market firms' international experience and home country characteristics are core sources of learning and constitute important determinants of emerging market firms' acquisition behaviour in developed countries. Rabbiosi's study of 808 south-north acquisitions undertaken in Europe, Japan, and North America by firms from the emerging economies of Brazil, Russia, India, and China showed that the acquisitions were conducted incrementally. Acquisition experience in developed markets increased the likelihood of exploitative expansion, whereas acquisition experience in developing markets did not appear to have any effect. The results also show that a lack of market and knowledge-based resources at home tended to curb explorative acquisitions by firms in emerging markets. Deng (2010) also pointed out that increasing numbers of Chinese enterprises regard cross-border M&As as a tool to obtain knowledge and strategic assets to enhance their competitiveness. Deng discussed this issue from the perspective of absorptive capacity, comparing striking international M&A transactions by Lenovo and TCL. Deng concluded that overseas M&As by Chinese enterprises are essentially influenced by the absorptive capacity of the acquirers.

An MNE's absorptive capacity is of strategic significance for its business operations in other emerging markets. Peng (2012) pointed out that Chinese managers tended to be unfamiliar with the rules of the game in the host country and not internationally savvy, and they had difficulty communicating seamlessly with local managers, employees, and politicians in the host country. Based on the literature, overseas work or study experience can help managers break through language barriers, improve the efficiency of their communication with local people, and become familiar with the trading rules in overseas markets, allowing them to make informed decisions about cross-border M&As. With more overseas experience, the board of directors can carry out more robust decision-making on cross-border M&As and exert a more positive effect on the corporate performance attributed to cross-border M&As.

In addition, the principal-agent theory holds that managers can obtain private benefits from international diversification and are therefore willing to pursue it even if shareholders' wealth could be reduced. The degree of internationalisation of enterprises is a complex decision variable. FDI strategies depend on the ability of enterprises to deal with information asymmetry and the potential agency conflicts with foreign investors. When FDI comes with a high requirement for information disclosure, it is characterised by a low frequency and long cycle, leading to agency problems. Under the agency framework, these problems involve adverse selection and moral hazard. Therefore, FDI decisions depend on corporate governance characteristics (Filatotchev et al., 2007). When enterprises invest in markets with legal and economic environments of various quality, their internationalisation efforts are affected by information asymmetry and persistent risks. The principal-agent theory holds that the governance relationship between the principal (shareholder) and the agent (senior management) may influence the FDI decisions of enterprises. Specific FDI decisions may be related to managers' risk preferences and decision-making horizons, and other main shareholder constituencies (Hoskisson & Hitt, 2002). FDI decisions depend on the parent company's ability to deal with information asymmetry and potential agency conflicts with foreign companies. The complexity of foreign markets increases the information processing needs of senior management and the information asymmetry between managers and shareholders, resulting in more principal-agent severe problems (Lu et al., 2009).

Executive pay is another important variable in corporate governance research. Studies have mostly focused on Western executive pay management, reflecting shareholders' efforts to alleviate agency problems by linking executive pay to shareholder returns. However, these studies have ignored the possibility of a causal relationship between incentive effectiveness and salary and corporate performance. Buck et al. (2008) studied the influence of board compensation on corporate performance in Chinese companies. They reported the sensitivity of firm performance to executive pay in China compared with other contexts and examined whether China's unique institutional environment produced outcomes consistent with those found in Western market economies. They found a causal relationship between corporate performance and executive pay in the form of rewards and incentives.

8.1.4 Stakeholders

The multinational governance of companies affects and is affected by many stakeholders. The relevant literature focuses on the opportunistic behaviour of ordinary employees, the host country's labour protection laws, and the psychic distance of the host country. Sun and Tobin (2005) conducted a case study on the state-owned Bank of China (Hong Kong) Limited and concluded that an overseas listing could effectively reduce the disorder of policies and management opportunism in the home country. During IPO preparation and the first two years of listing on the HKSE, the bank saw major upgrades in management and a significant improvement in corporate governance practices. Policy makers are more cautious about optimising policy choices when they think that the speculative behaviour of managers causes moral hazards. The legal system of the parent company is regulated and restricted by the rules of more developed capital markets.

The labour protection laws of host countries also affect the cross-border M&As of Chinese enterprises. Many countries have implemented labour acts and M&A control acts. M&As meeting certain conditions must be reviewed by relevant government agencies before being executed. Alimov (2015) considered the changes in country-level employment protection regulations as a source of plausibly exogenous variations in labour laws and found that these regulations played an important role in cross-border merger activities. Over the 1991–2009 period, countries that tightened employment regulations attracted more foreign acquirers, especially from countries with relatively more flexible labour regulations. Enterprises from countries with poor labour protections are more willing to invest in countries with better labour protection to realise institutional complementation. Industries with explicit labour protection laws are more likely to enable foreign acquirers to identify underpriced targets and improve productivity and labour skills. Because pro-labour reforms allow foreign acquirers to acquire more skilled and productive local firms, these transactions are associated with greater deal synergies and improved post-merger operating performance.

Research attention has been paid to the influence of interdisciplinary constructs of stakeholders on the multinational governance of Chinese MNEs. Blomkvist and Drogendijk (2013) examined the value of psychic distance and furthered theory construction in the internationalisation of Chinese enterprises by explaining the internationalisation path of enterprises from developed countries. The study also discussed whether psychic distance and its stimuli (differences in language, region, culture, economic development, political system, education, and geographical distance) could influence Chinese overseas investment. The hypotheses tested in this paper included the relationship between psychic distance and its stimuli and Chinese FDI. The study concluded that Chinese OFDI is influenced by an aggregate construct of psychic distance and by some (but not all) forms of psychic distance stimulus—in particular, similarities or differences regarding language and culture, the level of industrialisation, and the level of democracy. The findings suggest that psychic distance and its stimuli cannot be ignored as explanatory factors for Chinese OFDI and that the explanatory value of these constructs depends on the context of the phenomenon under study.

8.2 Governance Mechanism of Chinese MNEs

Studies have explored the internal and external governance mechanisms of Chinese MNEs. The internal governance mechanism mainly comprises the mechanism for the interactions between parent and subsidiary companies, and the external governance mechanism is influenced by the institutional environments of the home and host countries.

8.2.1 Internal Governance Mechanism of Chinese MNEs

An increasing number of studies have shown that the internal governance mechanism involves not only traditional means of governance, such as supervision, compensation, and incentives but also the operations of social networks. O'Donnell (2000) used agency theory as the basis for a model that predicts monitoring mechanisms and incentive compensation. O'Donnell argued that these mechanisms are insufficient for managing subsidiaries characterised by high levels of intra-firm international interdependence, which require social control mechanisms. The empirical results also suggest that agency theory is limited in its ability to explain the phenomena of foreign subsidiary control. In a case study of the parent-subsidiary ownership structure of Ghoshal & Bartlett (1990) put forward a network governance model for MNEs. Studies of the multinational investment network of Japanese enterprises have also found that by learning about foreign entry modes, enterprises gained competitive edges over local enterprises, and with ongoing investment, this learning behaviour spread throughout the cooperative network of enterprises (Chang, 1995; Ghoshal & Bartlett, 1990).

The parent-subsidiary relationship governance of Chinese MNEs has the structural characteristics of a network. For example, Li et al. (2013) discussed the influence of network embeddedness on the performance of subsidiaries of MNEs. This study established a conceptual framework of market orientation, embeddedness, autonomy, and the performance of subsidiaries of MNEs in emerging markets. According to the findings, internal and external embeddedness had different effects on the performance of export- and market-oriented subsidiaries. Based on a sample of 233 subsidiaries of Chinese MNEs, the study found that external embeddedness had a positive impact on the special resources of export- and market-oriented subsidiaries, and these special resources had a positive impact only on local market-oriented subsidiaries; in contrast, internal embeddedness had a negative impact on the special resources of both types of subsidiaries.

8.2.2 External Governance Mechanism of Chinese MNEs

As the multinational behaviour of Chinese MNEs is influenced simultaneously by the institutional environments of the home and host countries, MNEs have developed a unique external governance mechanism.

The influence of the home country's institutional environment on the governance of Chinese MNEs is visible in the literature in two aspects: the government's support for multinational business operation and the competitive pressures in the home market.

Firstly, the Chinese government's 'Go Out' policy has encouraged multinational governance among Chinese enterprises. Buckley et al. (2007) gave three special explanations (capital market imperfections, special ownership advantages, and institutional factors) for FDI by Chinese enterprises. Karolyi (2009) observed that the home government tended to encourage the M&A activities of politically connected enterprises while restricting similar behaviour among some enterprises without political connections to establish or maintain the connected firms' status of 'national champions'. Most of the firms involved in Chinese cross-border mergers and acquisitions (CBMA) were publicly listed companies with leading positions in their home markets. In China, most of the shares of listed companies are still controlled by the state (Lau et al., 2007). Therefore, the cross-border M&A business of state-owned enterprises in China has a growing trend.

MNEs need to adapt to the characteristics of the home and host country networks and properly allocate network resources to gain profits. Enterprises that are deeply embedded in the home country's political network have a larger scale and more complex operations, making them more capable of overcoming the resistance of external ownership to reduce various political and contractual risks (Sun et al., 2010). In a study of OFDI in the crude oil industry in China and Brazil, Carvalho and Goldstein (2009) identified the role of governments and technology in the internationalisation strategy of the oil firms from the two countries and found that Chinese enterprises were motivated to catch up in terms of technological capabilities when investing abroad. Child and Tse (2001) focused on institutional changes as the central and most consequential contextual elements of China's transition and posited that the identification of China's key institutional characteristics could benefit the development of multinational business. Wang et al. (2012) examined the driving forces behind the foreign investment of emerging market enterprises. Their study integrated the institutional theory, industrial organisation economics, and the resource-based view and contributed new insights at the organisation, industry, and country levels, identifying influences at different levels. Drawing on a database of large-scale Chinese enterprises, they found that the home government's support and the home country's industrial structure played a key role in OFDI. Technological and marketing resources were less important. The results of theoretical analyses and empirical studies show that differences in institutional and industrial environments drive Chinese enterprises' foreign investment.

Chi and Sun (2013) explored the effects of environmental factors on China's multinational trade. Previous studies of export market-oriented (EMO) behaviour in both Western and non-Western settings have examined the antecedent factors (i.e. organisational structure, export systems, export coordination, senior management factors, and export dependence) and moderating factors (i.e. environmental turbulence and export experience) of the institutional environment. Chi and Sun identified key antecedents (such as export reward and training systems, senior management support, and export dependence), confirmed the moderating effects of environment and experience, and explained a large percentage of the variance (78.3%) in international trade behaviours of Chinese enterprises. Lu et al. (2010) posited that supportive government policies positively impact Chinese enterprises' strategic asset-oriented and market-oriented FDI. Technology-based competitive edges and high R&D intensity levels may motivate enterprises to pursue strategic asset-oriented FDI and export experience and high-level domestic industry competition may drive enterprises to pursue market-oriented OFDI.

The competition environment and the development level of the capital market in the home country also impose pressure on external governance. Deng (2009) pointed out that increasing numbers of Chinese enterprises were obtaining strategic assets through cross-border M&As to compensate for their competitive disadvantages. Based on institutional theory, Deng proposed a resource-driven model for the cross-border M&As of Chinese enterprises. To endow the institutional framework with more explanatory power, Deng carried out a multiple-case study of three Chinese firms: TCL, BOE, and Lenovo. The findings show that the three firms made cross-border M&As to acquire strategic assets in the unique institutional environment of China. Wu and Chen (2014) examined how the institutional environment of the home country affects the overseas expansion of emerging market enterprises with a study of 921 Chinese enterprises from 1996 to 2000. The study found that a better-developed institutional environment in the home country promotes the expansion of emerging market enterprises into international markets that are more advanced than the home country. In contrast, institutional instability in the home country inhibits these enterprises' overseas expansion. The effect of the institutional environment in the home country depended on enterprise-specific levels of government ownership, with a high proportion of government ownership weakening the positive effect of the home country's institutional development on enterprises' propensity to expand to more developed foreign markets. Yiu et al. (2007) highlighted the role of the institutional environment in the home country in Chinese enterprises' cross-border M&As. They found that the ownership advantage of Chinese enterprises was positively correlated with the degree of internationalisation, and the industrial competition and export density of the home country exerted a moderating effect on this relationship. One of the motivations for cross-border M&As is to compensate for the institutional defects of the home country or an enterprise's inadequacies.

The host country's institutional environment also exerts external pressure. MNEs are subject to a new set of market relations when entering a new country and can thus have trouble adapting to a different competitive environment. Decision-making in the context of foreign business operations pivots on the governance and coordination of relationships with local stakeholders (Todeva, 2005). Buckley et al. (2007), using official Chinese ODI data collected between 1984 and 2001 to test their hypotheses, found that China's OFDI was related to the capital entry risk in the host country, cultural proximity, overall development level of the host country, local market size, geographical proximity (1984–1991), and local natural resource endowment (1992–2001). Zhang et al. (2011) studied how institutional factors affected Chinese enterprises' overseas acquisitions and held that a successful cross-border acquisition by a Chinese enterprise is an outcome of institutional contingencies at multiple levels. Using a dataset of Chinese cross-border acquisition deals, they concluded that the likelihood of a Chinese firm carrying out a successful overseas acquisition would be lower if the host country has a lower level of institutional quality. The target industry is sensitive to national security, and the acquirer is an SOE. Luo (2002) also emphasised the different influences of the host country's institutional environment on the internationalisation capability building of Chinese MNEs' subsidiaries using different entry modes. Among the environmental and organisational factors that affected the capability development and building of MNEs in complex foreign markets, Luo found that environmental complexity and industry uncertainty were negatively correlated with capability development and building. Business culture promoted capability development but not capability building. Capability development was related to the wholly owned entry mode and capability building to the joint venture mode. MNEs seeking domestic market expansion carried out more capability development and building than those seeking export market growth. It was further shown that the threat of environmental hazards to capability building diminished when the joint venture entry mode was used. Appropriate capability development and alliance building were found to enhance the performance of enterprises.

The level of resource richness of the host country also affects the multinational investment motivation of Chinese enterprises. Blonigen et al. (2014) pointed out that some enterprises seek competitive advantages by purposefully acquiring local enterprises with high productivity and high skills but have recently suffered from the negative effects of high productivity. Beule and Duanmu (2012) analysed a dataset of mergers and acquisitions in China and India. They found that acquisitions were more likely to occur in the mining industry in countries with underdeveloped institutions and rich resources and high-technology industries in countries with high institutional quality and rich strategic resources.

References

Alimov, A. (2015). Labour market regulations and cross-border mergers and acquisitions. *Journal of International Business Studies, 2*(16), 1–26.

Beule, F., & Duanmu, J. (2012). Locational determinants of internationalization: A firm-level analysis of Chinese and Indian acquisitions. *European Management Journal, 30*(3), 264–277.

Blomkvist, K., & Drogendijk, R. (2013). The impact of psychic distance on Chinese outward foreign direct investments. *Management International Review, 53*(5), 659–686.

Blonigen, B. A., Fontagne, L., Sly, N., & Toubal, F. (2014). Cherries for sale: The incidence and timing of cross-border M&A. *Journal of International Economics, 94*(2), 341–357.

Buck, T., Liu, X., & Skovoroda, R. (2008). Top executive pay and firm performance in China. *Journal of International Business Studies, 39*(5), 833–850.

Buckley, P. J., Clegg, L. J., Cross, A. R., Liu, X., Voss, H., & Zheng, P. (2007). The determinants of Chinese outward foreign direct investment. *Journal of International Business Studies, 38*(4), 499–518.

Carvalho, F., & Goldstein, A. (2009). *The 'making of' national giants: Technology and governments shaping the international expansion of oil companies from Brazil and China*. Multinationals and Emerging Economies, chapter 7, Edward Elgar.

Chang, S. J. (1995). International expansion strategy of Japanese firms: Capability building through sequential entry. *Academy of Management Journal, 2*(38), 383–407.

Chen, Y. Y., & Young, M. N. (2010). Cross-border mergers and acquisitions by Chinese listed companies: A principal–principal perspective. *Asia Pacific Journal of Management, 27*(3), 523–539.

Chi, T., & Sun, Y. (2013). Development of firm export market oriented behaviour: Evidence from an emerging economy. *International Business Review, 22*(1), 339–350.

Child, J., & Tse, D. K. (2001). China's transition and its implications for international business. *Journal of International Business Studies, 32*(1), 5–21.

Chua, R. Y. J., Morris, M. M., & Ingram, P. (2009). Guanxi vs networking: Distinctive configurations of affect- and cognition-based trust in the networks of Chinese vs American managers. *Journal of International Business Studies, 40*(3), 490–508.

Deng, P. (2009). Why do Chinese firms tend to acquire strategic assets in international expansion? *Journal of World Business, 44*(1), 74–84.

Deng, P. (2010). What determines performance of cross-border M&As by Chinese companies? An absorptive capacity perspective. *Thunderbird International Business Review, 52*(6), 509–524.

Filatotchev, I., Strange, R., Piesse, J., & Lien, Y. C. (2007). FDI by firms from newly industrialised economies in emerging markets: Corporate governance, entry mode and location. *Journal of International Business Studies, 38*(4), 556–572.

Ghoshal, S., & Bartlett, C. A. (1990). The multinational corporation as an interorganisational network. *Academy of Management Review, 15*(4), 603–625.

Hoskisson, R. E., & Hitt, M. A. (2002). Conflicting voices: The effects of institutional ownership heterogeneity and internal governance on corporate innovation strategies. *Academy of Management Journal, 4*(45), 697–716.

Hu, H. W., & Cui, L. (2014). Outward foreign direct investment of publicly listed firms from China: A corporate governance perspective. *International Business Review, 23*(4), 750–760.

Ji, J. M., & Dimitratos, P. (2013). An empirical investigation into international entry mode decision-making effectiveness. *International Business Review, 22*(6), 994–1007.

Karolyi, G. (2009). *What is different about governmentcontrolled acquirers in cross-border acquisitions?* [EB/OL]. https://www.econstor.eu/bitstream/10419/43545/1/640343694.pdf

Lau, C. M., Fan, D. K. K., Young, M. N., & Wu, S. (2007). Corporate governance effectiveness during institutional transition. *International Business Review, 16,* 425–448.

Li, X. Y., Liu, X. M., & Thomas, H. (2013). Market orientation, embeddedness and the autonomy and performance of multinational subsidiaries in an emerging economy. *Management International Review, 53*(6), 869–897.

Lu, J., Liu, X., & Wang, H. (2010). Motives for outward FDI of Chinese private firms: Firm resources, industry dynamics, and government policies. *Management and Organisation Review, 7*(2), 223–248.

Lu, J. Y., Bin, X., & Liu, X. H. (2009). The effects of corporate governance and institutional environments on export behaviour in emerging economies. *Management International Review, 49*(4), 455–478.

Luo, Y. (2002). Capability exploitation and building in a foreign market: Implications for multinational enterprises. *Organisation Science, 13*(1), 48–63.

Morck, R., Yeung, B., & Zhao, M. (2008). Perspectives on China's outward foreign direct investment. *Journal of International Business Studies, 39*(3), 337–350.

Ning, L., Kuo, J., Strange, R., & Wang, B. (2014). International investors' reactions to cross-border acquisitions by emerging market multinationals. *International Business Review, 23*(4), 811–823.

O'Donnell, S. W. (2000). Managing foreign subsidiaries: Agents of headquarters, or an interdependent network? *Strategic Management Journal, 21*(5), 525–548.

Peng, M. W. (1997). Firm growth in transitional economies: Three longitudinal cases from China. *Organisation Studies, 3*(18), 385–413.

Peng, M. W. (2012). The global strategy of emerging multinationals from China. *Global Strategy Journal, 2*(2), 97–107.

Peng, M. W., & Luo, Y. D. (2000). Managerial ties and firm performance in a transition economy: The nature of a micro-macro link. *Academy of Management Journal, 3*(43), 486–501.

Rabbiosi, A. P. L., Elia, A. P. S., & Bertoni, A. P. F. (2012). Acquisitions by EMNCs in developed markets. *Management International Review, 52*(2), 193–212.

Sun, L. X., & Tobin, D. (2005). International listing as a mechanism of commitment to more credible corporate governance practices: The case of the Bank of China (Hong Kong). *Corporate Governance: An International Review, 13*(1), 81–91.

Sun, P., Mellahi, K., & Thun, E. (2010). The dynamic value of MNE political embeddedness: The case of the Chinese automobile industry. *Journal of International Business Studies, 41*(7), 1161–1182.

Todeva, E. (2005). Governance control and coordination in network context: The cases of Japanese Keiretsu and Sogo Shosha. *Journal of International Management, 11*(1), 87–109.

Wang, C., Hong, J., Kafouros, M., & Boateng, A. (2012). What drives outward FDI of Chinese firms? Testing the explanatory power of three theoretical frameworks. *International Business Review, 21*(3), 425–438.

Wu, J., & Chen, X. (2014). Home country institutional environments and foreign expansion of emerging market firms. *International Business Review, 23*(5), 862–872.

Xie, Y. H., & Lyn, S. A. (2009). Social networks and the internationalisation of Chinese entrepreneurs. *Global Business and Organisational Excellence, 29*(1), 61–78.

Yiu, D. W., Lau, C. M., & Bruton, G. D. (2007). International venturing by emerging economy firms: The effects of firm capabilities, home country networks, and corporate entrepreneurship. *Journal of International Business Studies, 38*(4), 519–540.

Zhang, J., Zhou, C., & Ebbers, H. (2011). Completion of Chinese overseas acquisitions: Institutional perspectives and evidence. *International Business Review, 20*(2), 226–238.

CHAPTER 9

Path and Characteristics of the Multinational Governance of Chinese Enterprises

Since the founding of the People's Republic of China in 1949, Chinese enterprises have developed rapidly. The number of Chinese enterprises in the world's 500 largest companies reached 120 in 2018. Chinese enterprises have gradually gained their footing in the international market, and their efforts to globalise have come to fruition. Through continuous internationalisation, Chinese enterprises have improved their multinational governance ability and enhanced their competitiveness and global influence. In enterprise internationalisation, increasing research efforts have been devoted to corporate governance, which has become a crucial influencing factor in the choice of host country and entry mode and the acquisition of legitimacy for local operations. The history of business internationalisation in both Chinese and foreign contexts reveals that multinational corporate governance is a key to global success, which makes research into multinational governance increasingly important. This chapter outlines the path and characteristics of the multinational corporate governance of Chinese enterprises through an analysis of their internationalisation process, drawing on theories of multinational corporate governance.

© The Author(s), under exclusive license to Springer Nature Singapore Pte Ltd. 2022
R. Lin and J. J. Chen, *The Theory and Application of Multinational Corporate Governance*, https://doi.org/10.1007/978-981-16-7703-8_9

9.1 Process and Theoretical Development of China's Multinational Corporate Governance

9.1.1 Process of China's Multinational Corporate Governance

Multinational corporate governance deals with issues arising in the business activities of MNEs. Corporate governance is a set of institutional arrangements based on scientific decision-making designed to coordinate the relationships between stakeholders, of which shareholders are at the core. Multinational corporate governance refers to arrangements dealing with such issues as the duties and power of management and shareholders of a parent company and its subsidiaries within MNEs. Multinational governance is not simply an extension of domestic corporate governance but rather a distinctive outcome of technological, organisational, and institutional factors. One of its major features is the expansion of stakeholders. As MNEs carry out business in more locations than domestic corporations, their multinational scale, scope, and influence bring in many potential stakeholders, including the host and home country governments, parent companies, subsidiaries, and partners. The dynamic interactions among these stakeholders make multinational corporate governance distinctive from the governance of a company operating only domestically. Therefore, the analysis of multinational corporate governance processes accounting for different stakeholders and the distinctive way that MNEs operate is needed to reveal the path of multinational corporate governance.

9.1.1.1 The Role of Government

Due to China's unique national conditions and pattern of economic development, the Chinese government has played important role in the development of Chinese MNEs and is the key stakeholder affecting their multinational governance. Therefore, changes in the government's role reflect the evolution in the multinational corporate governance of Chinese MNEs.

To summarise, the multinational corporate governance of Chinese MNEs, driven by continuous policy shifts, has evolved from administrative-led pilot projects to business-led practices, with the latter drawing increasing attention as China's multinational business activities have increased. This process can be divided into two stages based on the changing role of government.

1. 1978–2000: Loosened Restrictions

From 1978 to 2000, China focused on obtaining outside resources for its foreign policies and lacked a sound legal system to guide and encourage Chinese corporations to globalise. During this period, the government attached more importance to attracting foreign investment in domestic companies while loosening its restrictions and providing step-by-step guidance on MNEs' external governance.

The reform and opening-up strategy were implemented by the Chinese central government in 1978, marking China's initial steps to open up the economy to foreign trade and investment and encourage domestic companies to engage in multinational business. This policy created an external environment within which Chinese MNEs could globalise and laid the foundation for China's multinational corporate governance studies. In August 1979, the State Council proposed start business abroad, marking the first time China had loosened regional restrictions on business and allowed domestic companies to carry out business outside China. Chinese multinational corporate business thus began. In 1982, the Ministry of Foreign Trade and Economic Cooperation (MOFTEC) was established to review and manage Chinese companies' overseas investments, ensuring that multinational corporate business was under the regulation and guidance of a specialised department. From that point, the Chinese government gradually relaxed its restrictions on Chinese companies' global operations. In 1992, the China Securities Regulatory Commission (CSRC) was founded. Domestic companies were allowed to enter foreign capital markets through IPOs and to raise funds in international markets. Restrictions were also eased on the equity of MNEs. The Export–Import Bank of China (China Eximbank) was established in 1994 to provide credit support for various forms of outward investment and cooperation and special loans made available for overseas investments. In May 1997, the Ministry of Commerce (MOFCOM) issued the *Interim Regulations on the Establishment of Overseas Trading Companies and Representative Offices*, allowing corporations to establish trading companies and representative offices outside of China. In February 1999, the State Council released the *Notice of the General Office of the State Council Transmitting the Opinions of the Ministry of Foreign Trade and Economic Cooperation, the State Economic and Trade Commission, and the Ministry of Finance on Encouraging Companies to Carry Out Processing and Assembling Business Overseas* to allow companies to 'go global' with overseas processing business.

With these steps, the government progressively relaxed the restrictions on multinational Chinese companies and set up a specialised department to guide multinational business. The ways of expanding abroad also diversified. It also became easier for foreign investment to enter the Chinese market, as evidenced by the proportion of foreign-owned equities. Before 1991, the government encouraged joint ventures and partnerships between foreign investors and domestic companies, especially SOEs, while reining in wholly foreign-owned companies. After 1992, the relaxed restrictions on foreign investment into China led to a growing number of foreign MNEs expanding into China, which to some extent developed China's multinational corporate governance. Chinese companies obtained experience and knowledge through cooperation with foreign-owned companies in China, which helped them prepare for their march into the international market.

2. 2001 Onwards: Strong Support

China became a member of the World Trade Organisation (WTO) in 2001 and has since upheld 'going global' as a national strategy under the guidance of the CPC Central Committee and the State Council. Accordingly, a set of policies have been put in place to encourage, promote, and support Chinese companies' multinational business in terms of strategies, foreign exchanges, approval procedures, financial assistance, and macro guidance, forming a relatively complete policy system (see Table 9.1 for details). At this stage, the Chinese government, as a major stakeholder in Chinese multinational corporate governance, provided strong support for the multinational business of Chinese companies. Thanks to these favourable policies, Chinese MNEs began to take the initiative in their pursuit of international business rather than merely following the government's lead. An increasing variety of business entities engaged in multinational business emerged, including private companies that embraced different ways of doing business.

It was also during this period that studies of multinational governance began to draw more attention. The government became aware of the impact of multinational corporate governance on business activities and began to pursue higher levels of multinational governance in Chinese companies. In 2003, the State-Owned Assets Supervision and Administration Commission (SASAC) and the Organisation Department of the

Table 9.1 The changing role of government in China's multinational corporate governance

Date	Government policy	Impact of change in government's role on multinational governance
December 1978	The reform and opening-up strategy were rolled out at the 3rd Plenary Session of the 11th CPC Central Committee	China begins to open up for international business operations
August 1979	The State Council proposed the 'permission to start a business abroad'	China's Multinational corporate operations begin
March 1982	MOFTEC established	Presence of a new ministry responsible for reviewing and managing Chinese companies' overseas investment
October 1992	CSRC founded	Domestic companies allowed to enter overseas capital markets through IPOs
1994	China Eximbank established	Credit support made available for various forms of outward investment and cooperation; special loans available for overseas investment
May 1997	MOFCOM issued the *Interim Regulations on the Establishment of Overseas Trading Companies and Representative Offices*	Corporations allowed to establish trading companies and representative offices outside China
February 1999	*Notice of the General Office of the State Council Transmitting the Opinions of the Ministry of Foreign Trade and Economic Cooperation, the State Economic and Trade Commission, and the Ministry of Finance on Encouraging Companies to Carry Out Processing and Assembling Business Overseas*	Companies encouraged to 'go global' with overseas processing business
2001	'Going global' strategy included in the *Outline of the Tenth Five-Year Plan for National Economic and Social Development*	Multinational business operations upgraded to the level of a national strategy

(continued)

Table 9.1 (continued)

Date	Government policy	Impact of change in government's role on multinational governance
October 2002	Foreign exchange administration reform	Companies operating abroad allowed to retain their profits instead of repatriating their funds
January 2003	The SASAC and the Organisation Department of the CPC Central Committee launched the first global recruitment of seven senior executives for central SOEs	An upsurge in global hiring of senior executives for central SOEs
March 2003	Foreign exchange risk reviews for foreign investment and the deposit for profit repatriation cancelled	Restrictions on foreign exchange purchases for outward investment relaxed
2003	MOFCOM begins to release the annual *Foreign Market Access Report*	Macro guidance provided for China's Multinational business operations
June 2004	The SASAC of the State Council issued the *Guidance on the Construction of the Board of Directors of Wholly State-Owned Companies (Trial)*	Outside directors could be hired from both inside and outside China; the employment of independent directors with overseas backgrounds was a highlight
October 2004	Overseas investment subject to approval instead of a review and a credit support mechanism for overseas investment was created	Restrictions on Multinational business further loosened and financial support provided
2004	MOFCOM begins to issue the *Catalogue of Industries by Country/Region for Guiding Outward Investment*	Macro guidance provided
2005	China Export & Credit Insurance Corporation begins to release the annual *Handbook of Country Risk*	Companies aided in analysing risks in different host countries to facilitate Multinational business
June 2006	Quotas of foreign exchange purchases were cancelled	Delegation of the power to review the source of foreign exchange funds in overseas investment

(continued)

Table 9.1 (continued)

Date	Government policy	Impact of change in government's role on multinational governance
January 2008	Taxation support (such as overseas income tax credits) introduced	Financial support
March 2009	Power of approval delegated, and approval procedures of overseas investment simplified	Greater convenience
2009	MOFCOM began to issue the *Outward Investment Cooperation Guidelines by Country/Region*	Host country guidelines available to assist companies in preparation for operations abroad
December 2012	Cross-border payment procedures simplified; some MNEs allowed to conduct two-way allocation of cross-border funds through short-term transactions	
September 2014	Overseas investment management model, combining filing and approval processes established	Clarified the principal role of companies in overseas investment activities; companies allowed to leverage their advantages to carry out overseas investment cooperation

CPC Central Committee launched the first global recruitment of seven senior executives for central SOEs, leading to a wave of international executive recruitment. In June 2004, the SASAC issued the *Guidance on the Construction of the Board of Directors of Wholly State-Owned Companies (Trial)*, which stated that outside directors could be hired from both inside and outside China. The employment of independent directors with overseas backgrounds was a highlight of this reform. These measures greatly improved Chinese companies' multinational governance structure and capabilities, taking their competitiveness and international influence to a higher level. The changing role of government in China's multinational corporate governance is summarised in Table 9.1.

9.1.1.2 The Role of Companies

Although the government plays a major role in multinational corporate governance, it is the companies that operate abroad. A company's multinational governance process is manifested in its multinational business activities and decision-making processes. A better understanding of

MNEs' business activities, decision-making, and structural changes can shed light on China's multinational corporate governance practices.

In November 1979, as the government began to relax restrictions on multinational business, Beijing Friendship Commercial Services Co. Ltd. and Tokyo Maruichi Shoji Co. Ltd. founded Kyowa Co. Ltd. in Tokyo as China's first multinational company engaged in non-import/export business; this marked China's first overseas joint venture and the inauguration of multinational business after the opening-up policy. A growing number of Chinese companies have since moved into international markets in various ways. Before 2000, the government focused on bringing in resources and left some limits on multinational business. During that period, all outward investments made by Chinese companies, regardless of the amount or method (M&As or IPOs), required approval from the State Council. With the absence of a sound management system, this requirement meant that only a small number of Chinese companies could globalise. In contrast, extensive foreign investment was attracted into the Chinese market for cooperation with domestic companies. For instance, American Motors Corporation (AMC) established Beijing Jeep Co. Ltd. as a Sino–US joint venture in January 1984; France Peugeot and International Finance Corporation (IFC) founded the Guangzhou Peugeot Automobile Company (GPAC) in March 1985; and US$180 million was invested by SAIC Motor and Volkswagen in September 1984 to set up SAIC Volkswagen Automotive Co. Ltd. as a Sino–German 50/50 joint venture. Foreign investment also brought opportunities for Chinese companies to enhance their multinational governance capabilities and accumulate experience for their subsequent move into the global arena. Thus, in this period, Chinese companies passively conducted multinational governance.

Multinational corporate governance has developed based on general corporate governance. China's corporate governance regime did not take shape until the mid-1980s, so multinational governance drew little attention until then. Later, multinational corporate governance came into the spotlight with the parallel development of corporate governance and multinational business. Based on certain milestones (see Table 9.2), China's multinational corporate governance development can be divided into four periods, as follows.

Table 9.2 Milestones in Chinese MNEs' multinational corporate governance

Period	Date	Milestones
1978–2000 Passive Multinational governance	November 1979	Beijing Friendship Commercial Services Co. Ltd. and Tokyo Maruichi Shoji Co. Ltd. found Kyowa Co. Ltd. in Tokyo, China's first overseas joint venture
	January 1984	Bank of China and China Resources jointly acquire Conic Investment Co. Ltd., Hong Kong's largest listed electronics company, marking the first overseas M&A deal by a Chinese company
	October 1992	Brilliance Auto goes public in New York, becoming the first Chinese company listed overseas
	July 1993	Tsingtao Brewery is listed in Hong Kong, and eight SOEs, including Shanghai Petrochemical and Maanshan Iron & Steel, go public overseas in the same year, bringing an upsurge in overseas IPOs by Chinese companies
	April 1999	Haier Group establishes Haier Industrial Park in South Carolina, becoming the first Chinese company to undertake greenfield investment in the US
Since 2001 Active Multinational governance	August 2001	Wanxiang Group invest US$28 billion to purchase Universal Automotive Industries Inc., a US-listed company, becoming the first private Chinese company to enter the US market through acquisitions
	November 2003	PICC Property and Casualty is listed in Hong Kong and China Life goes public in the US and Hong Kong, thus promoting the overseas listings of Chinese financial institutions

(continued)

Table 9.2 (continued)

Period	Date	Milestones
	January 2003	The SASAC and the Organisation Department of the CPC Central Committee launch the first global recruitment for seven senior executives for central SOEs, leading to a wave of international executive recruitment
	December 2004	Lenovo Group acquires IBM's global PC business with cash and stock and thus became the world's third-largest PC manufacturer
	2005	Large SOEs, such as Bank of Communications, China Construction Bank, and Shenhua Energy, successfully launch IPOs in Hong Kong
	November 2005	SINOSURE use a debt-to-equity swap for the first time and take control of the US company by sending four Chinese representatives to the board of directors
	December 2005	China Wuxi Suntech Power Co. Ltd. become the first private Chinese public to be listed on the NYSE
	February 2008	China Development Bank (CDB) participate in strategic projects such as China–Russian oil, China–Pakistan oil, and China–Turkey natural gas projects by providing loans in exchange for resources
	September 2008	Zoomlion and three other institutions, including Hony Capital, acquire the Italian company CIFA in the first offshore private equity (PE) investment by Chinese companies
	April 2011	Huawei sets up its first overseas board of directors in its Australian subsidiary, which comprises Australians with business and political experience

(continued)

Table 9.2 (continued)

Period	Date	Milestones
	May 2012	Dalian Wanda Group purchases AMC Theatres in the US, the world's second-largest movie theatre chain, in the largest acquisition deal by a Chinese private company in the US
	October 2015	A Chinese corporate consortium led by China Railway Corporation signs a contract for Indonesia's Jakarta–Bandung high-speed railway project, taking China's high-speed rail industry global for the first time
	February 2016	ChemChina acquires Syngenta, a Swiss agrochemical and seed company, for US$43 billion, in the largest overseas acquisition by a Chinese company
	December 2016	Chongqing Casin Group acquires the Chicago Stock Exchange (CHX) in a pioneering purchase of US stock exchanges by Chinese investors

1. *1979–1991*

After the reform and opening-up policy, China began to embrace multinational business, and some Chinese companies began to participate in overseas operations. For example, in 1984, Bank of China and China Resources jointly acquired Conic Investment Co. Ltd., which was then Hong Kong's largest listed electronics company. This was the first overseas cross-border M&A deal completed by a Chinese company. However, the government still wielded tight control over Chinese companies' outward investment activities, which were then subject to strict reviews. Only a small number of companies, mostly SOEs, were engaged in multinational business. Corporate governance was a fledgling concept, and the value of multinational governance had not been recognised. The focus of consideration by the domestic government was whether a planned economy or a market economy would be more effective. The

Chinese government had not devised a clear plan for a socialist market economy. As foreign-owned companies were mainly partnered with SOEs in China, foreign-owned equities were still under strict restrictions. For Chinese companies, the main task at this stage was to gain knowledge and experience from cooperation with foreign-owned companies that had entered the Chinese market under the guidance of the government and improve their multinational governance capabilities to prepare for global expansion.

2. 1992–2000

In 1992, the government loosened restrictions on domestic foreign-owned equities and allowed Chinese companies to raise funds in international markets through IPOs. This policy brought about an upsurge in overseas IPOs by Chinese companies. In October 1992, Brilliance Auto went public on the New York Stock Exchange (NYSE), becoming the first Chinese company listed overseas. Increasing numbers of Chinese companies followed its lead in entering overseas markets through IPOs. For instance, Tsingtao Brewery was listed in Hong Kong in July 1993; in the same year, eight SOEs went public overseas, including Shanghai Petrochemical and Maanshan Iron & Steel. However, the companies listed during this period were mainly SOEs in manufacturing and infrastructure, the pillars of the national economy. Their listings were primarily driven by the efforts of the Chinese government and the rapid development of the national economy in the 1990s. In general, although breakthroughs were made in overseas listings, only a small number of companies and sectors were involved. Between 1992 and 2000, Chinese companies were still beginners in multinational M&As, with the number of cross-border M&As deals completed by Chinese companies annually accounting for less than 1% of the world's total.

Nonetheless, during this time, Chinese companies made significant strides towards a new stage in multinational business. As China attracted foreign investment and relaxed its restrictions on foreign-owned equities, more Chinese companies entered overseas markets in various ways, turning from product exports to capital operations as a means of conducting multinational business. As Chinese companies were still in the initial stages of international expansion, there were few studies on

Chinese multinational corporate governance compared with international trade and foreign investment.

3. 2001–2007

After China joined the WTO in 2001, the government started to encourage Chinese companies to 'go global'. With China's transition from a planned economy to a market economy, a rapidly growing number of Chinese companies began to carry out multinational business activities in a greater breadth of industries. The IT industry and private sector began to stand out in this regard. In August 2001, Wanxiang Group acquired Universal Automotive Industries Inc., a US-listed company, in a deal worth US$28 billion, becoming the first private Chinese company to enter the US market through acquisition. In December 2004, Lenovo Group purchased IBM's personal computing division, which included the ThinkPad line, for US$650 million in cash and US$600 million in Lenovo Group shares. This purchase had a tremendous impact on China and the rest of the world, with Lenovo becoming a world-class manufacturer of laptop computers. In November 2003, PICC Property and Casualty was listed in Hong Kong, and China Life went public in the US and Hong Kong, which promoted the overseas listing of Chinese financial institutions. In 2005, some large SOEs, including the Bank of Communications, China Construction Bank, and Shenhua Energy, successfully launched IPOs in Hong Kong. In October of that year, China Wuxi Suntech Power Co. Ltd. became the first private Chinese company listed on the NYSE. In October 2007, the Industrial and Commercial Bank of China bought a 20% stake in the Standard Bank of South Africa, the largest bank in Africa, for US$5.46 billion, and thus became the bank's largest shareholder with the largest multinational acquisition by a Chinese company.

This period saw rapid advances in the multinational operation capabilities of Chinese companies, and the government and corporations paid increasing attention to cross-border business. The number of overseas listings rose steadily, from 18 in 2001 to 105 in 2007. Outward investment gradually increased through M&As and greenfield investment. In addition, the main targets for M&As were no longer limited to small and medium-sized foreign enterprises but included world-class companies and even industry leaders. Major takeovers by Chinese companies considerably raised China's global influence.

However, with their increasing involvement in multinational business, Chinese companies encountered more problems related to multinational governance. Increasing numbers of Chinese companies failed or floundered abroad, leaving many multinational failures during this period. For example, in March 2004, American investors sued China Life for information disclosure issues; in April 2004, TCL encountered cultural adaptability issues after it took over Thomson's colour TV business; in August 2006, SAIC Motor experienced strikes after it acquired South Korea's SsangYong Motor Company; in 2007, Ping An Insurance lost nearly RMB 24 billion from its investment in Fortis Belgium. These events made the government and companies realise the importance of multinational governance. Because China lagged behind Western developed countries in corporate governance, Chinese companies encountered many governance problems when they entered Western markets. To boost multinational business, the government and companies began to focus on improving corporate governance by enhancing compliance and aligning with international standards. As part of such efforts, an increasing number of Chinese companies introduced international professionals with overseas backgrounds or international experience into their boards of directors and senior management. For example, Geely began to invite personnel with international experience into its board of directors in 2004 to ensure better decision-making in its international business. This practice also helped Chinese MNEs to reduce the difference in governance levels when they entered foreign markets, facilitating their efforts to gain legitimacy.

4. *From 2007 Onwards*

The global financial crisis of 2008 dealt a severe blow to the multinational business of Chinese companies. The downturn in foreign economies was directly reflected in Chinese companies' behaviour in the international market, as seen in the number of overseas listings. In 2008, only 52 Chinese companies were listed overseas, less than half of the number in 2007. After a subsequent bounce-back, followed by a decline in 2011 due to the European debt crisis, the number rebounded in 2013. However, the global economic downturn after 2007 also produced M&A opportunities for Chinese MNEs. As a result, rapid growth was observed in overseas listings after 2007, with outward investment increasing year by year. The number of outward investment deals worth more than US$100 million was 27 in 2007, 38 in 2008, 65 in 2009, 73 in 2010, 100 in 2011, 120 in 2012, 112 in 2013, 147 in 2014, 156 in 2015, 765 in 2016, and 431 in 2017.

During this period, the multinational operation capabilities of Chinese companies improved. Both industry and academia came to realise the importance of multinational corporate governance due to problems arising from multinational practices and made efforts to solve these through corporate governance. In addition, multinational corporate governance was further classified into parent company governance and subsidiary governance, with the host country, home country, and MNE identified as three basic governance dimensions. The significant influence of differences in multinational institutions and cultures on multinational business has gradually come to the fore in the literature. A growing number of scholars have studied the multinational operation process using the corporate governance theory, institutional theory, and internationalisation theory and have focused on host country selection, foreign market entry mode (especially equity entry mode) selection, multinational governance mode, and the acquisition of legitimacy.

As the multinational business expands, more attention is being paid to Chinese multinational corporate governance, and studies on this topic have become increasingly focused on specific issues. Chinese companies have experienced internationalisation from the start and deepened their knowledge of multinational governance during their handling of management challenges in this process. Although China's multinational governance needs further improvement, the progress made and the increasing global influence of Chinese companies should be acknowledged, as shown by the number of Chinese companies listed in the Fortune 500 leaping from only 3 in 1995 to 115 in 2017 and 120 in 2018. These facts further verify the role of multinational governance in multinational business. Companies must sharpen their multinational governance capabilities to achieve long-term development.

9.1.2 Theoretical Development of Multinational Governance

MNEs are now playing an increasingly dominant role in steering the global economy. As MNEs first appeared in Western capitalist countries, research into MNEs emerged abroad earlier than in China. Hymer's (1960) monopolistic advantage theory, Vernon's (1966) product life cycle theory, Buckley and Casson's (1976) internalisation theory, and Dunning's (1977) eclectic theory of international production all explained the international business activities of MNEs from different perspectives. As these theories gained in popularity, corporate governance became of greater interest to researchers examining the issues encountered by MNEs during multinational operations. Multinational governance theory refers to applying corporate governance theory to the international business activities of MNEs and deals with how to carry out international and multinational business better. It thus differs from previous internationalisation-related theories, which focused on explaining why international and multinational business is important.

Multinational corporate governance is interrelated with international business operations. With the development of multinational businesses and internationalisation, multinational corporate governance has drawn more attention. As shown in the milestones of Chinese MNEs' multinational development, the multinational business of Chinese MNEs is expanding. Multinational governance issues deserve more attention as internationalisation deepens, and there has been an increasing body of research and analysis in this regard. Studies of China's multinational corporate governance have advanced with the evolution of multinational business. In the beginning, researchers were mostly focused on the effects of overseas business activities on MNEs, such as increases in company competitiveness and global influence. With MNEs gaining a more profound knowledge of multinational governance as they have extended their global reach, researchers began to focus on specific multinational business activities, such as host country and entry mode selection, the localised business in host countries and acquiring legitimacy.

Multinational corporate governance can be divided into internal and external governance. The former focuses on the governance of MNEs' structure and internal relationships. As companies grow their multinational business, they increase their investments in host countries and obtain more local experience and knowledge. Sales subsidiaries are often set up for localised operations. At this point, building an appropriate governance structure for managing the relationship between a parent company and its subsidiaries becomes important. As multinational operations are intended for direct manufacturing and production in host countries, MNEs should also consider the governance of external stakeholders, institutional and cultural influences, and how to realise localisation. In the case of Chinese companies, most studies have emphasised the factors that influence decision-making in multinational operations, mainly from the perspective of internationalisation and foreign trade and investment, with fewer being concerned with Chinese multinational corporate governance.

9.2 Evolution of China's Multinational Corporate Governance

Based on multinational business activities, the evolution of Chinese multinational corporate governance has involved drivers of multinational business, host country selection, entry mode selection, parent company and subsidiary governance modes, and MNEs' governance structures.

9.2.1 Development of Drivers of International Business

The drivers of multinational expansion for Chinese MNEs have changed constantly during internationalisation and with the growth of their competitiveness. There has been a general shift from an administrative-led model to business-led multinational governance, attributable to China's economic restructuring from a planned economy to a market economy. At the beginning of the reform and opening up, Chinese companies relied mostly on exporting products at a low cost. With the continuous growth of China's economy, Chinese MNEs improved their competitiveness and looked to the international market for more resources, partly out of a desire to avoid intense domestic competition.

Since the beginning of the twenty-first century, many more Chinese companies have entered the international capital market. Low-cost resources and economies of scale are no longer the only motivations for internationalisation. Instead, strategies are taken into consideration to solve multinational operational problems and enhance MNEs' influence. Strategic resources and efficiency have thus become major drivers. Tian et al. (2007) explored Chinese companies' behaviour and path selection in their internationalisation by conducting a content analysis based on the main theories of the internationalisation of foreign companies. The results show that resources and markets were the driving forces for Chinese companies' internationalisation in the early stages, but the main drivers have since shifted to strategic assets and efficiency. Analysing the driving forces of Chinese companies' international expansion based on a sample of the top 500 Chinese companies in 2007, Xiong and Deng (2010) found that MNEs mainly aimed to seek larger potential in the early stages of

Table 9.3 Changes in the driving forces of Chinese MNEs' multinational operations

Period	Markets		Resources		Strategic assets		Efficiency	
	Number	Proportion (%)	Number	Proportion (%)	Number	Proportion (%)	Number	Proportion (%)
1987–1998	39	40.21	27	27.84	16	16.49	15	15.46
1999–2001	68	31.63	35	16.27	54	25.12	58	26.98
2002–2007	76	23.46	47	14.51	103	31.79	98	30.25

internationalisation foreign markets and low-cost resources. As internationalisation continued, MNEs shifted their focus to strategic assets (such as international brand building and long-term strategies for the parent company) and sought to achieve economies of scale and economies of scope through the rationalisation of production. Strategic assets became a major driver of multinational business for Chinese companies in the twenty-first century. Some data to support this shift are presented in Table 9.3.

The evolution of multinational business operations has seen a diversification of the driving forces for Chinese MNEs. Primarily since the beginning of the twenty-first century, when there was a major improvement in their competitiveness, Chinese MNEs have increasingly conducted multinational business activities based on their needs, as reflected in their internationalisation strategies.

9.2.2 Changes in the Host Country Selection

Concerning host countries, the overseas market regions preferred by Chinese MNEs are Southeast Asia, North America, and the European Union (EU), which are in descending order according to psychic distance. Their first choices are Hong Kong and Southeast Asia, where market conditions and cultures are similar to those in China, followed by North America and Europe. Their outward investment focuses on developing economies, particularly in Asia. Investment in developed economies, especially in the EU, North America, and Oceania, has risen yearly since 2000 (Figs. 9.1 and 9.2).

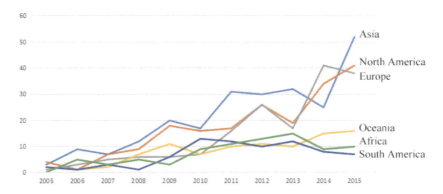

Fig. 9.1 Changes in the number of host countries for investment, 2005–2015

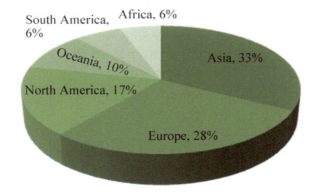

Fig. 9.2 Geographical distribution of China's outward investment in 2015

With regard to the geographical distribution of multinational investment, Hong Kong and the US are the most favoured host economies for both foreign companies and Chinese MNEs. Hong Kong enjoys geographical and cultural advantages for hosting Chinese companies. The US, the most developed country, is a target market for Chinese companies because of its well-developed capital market, which allows these companies to improve their governance mechanisms and expand their influence. The choice of host countries also varies depending on the driving forces of MNEs' multinational operations. Due to China's institutional surplus with African countries, India, and most Southeast Asian countries, including Thailand and Indonesia, market resources and costs are the first consideration in selecting these host economies for Chinese MNEs looking to seize local product markets. However, considering China's institutional deficit with the US and the EU, Chinese MNEs choose these markets mainly to improve their strategic influence. The number of target host countries has expanded as Chinese companies continue to increase their competitiveness.

The first step for MNEs to globalise is to select a host country. To survive in a new environment, they must pay attention to foreign market entry factors, especially the institutional and cultural differences between the home and host countries. The rising number of host countries in which Chinese companies operate multinational business not only represents an improved capability to handle institutional gaps but also demonstrates deeper insights into multinational governance, which help them to understand the effects of institutional and cultural differences on multinational operations. Moreover, with the development of corporate competitiveness, different driving forces affect MNEs' choice of the host country, as suggested by the fact that Chinese MNEs have entered numerous host economies with which China has an institutional surplus and those with which it has a deficit.

9.2.3 Changes in the Entry Modes

The next important step in internationalisation is to select an entry mode. Foreign market entry modes are commonly seen as institutional arrangements through which MNEs transfer their products, human resources, technologies, management experience, and other resources to other countries (Huang & Liu, 2009). From the perspective of management and operations, host country market entry modes can be categorised into trade, contractual, and investment modes (Zhang & Xu, 2008). According to MOFCOM, Chinese companies' foreign market entry modes include establishing new companies (wholly owned companies, subsidiaries, and joint ventures), acquisition (multinational M&As), overseas branches (branches, representative offices, and local offices), and project contracting (mainly international contracts in construction and engineering). Entry modes can also be divided into equity and non-equity modes.

According to internationalisation theory, multinational business activities are accompanied by increasing demand for resources. Generally, export entry modes require the fewest resources, followed by acquisitions, joint ventures, and subsidiaries. A company, therefore, should expand its multinational operations in this order. As resource commitments increase, the entry modes of Chinese MNEs generally evolve from export to acquisition to joint ventures and subsidiaries and finally to overseas listings.

Chinese MNEs are increasingly opting for equity entry modes as their multinational business grows, and they have been conducting active multinational governance since the beginning of the twenty-first century. Equity entry modes involve wholly owned companies and joint ventures. Chinese MNEs should decide the appropriate modes based on institutional distance, cultural distance, diversification strategies, and corporate governance structure. For example, they can start wholly owned companies in host countries featuring a large institutional deficit or launch joint ventures in host countries featuring a large institutional surplus.

Overall, as the Chinese economy and MNEs grow, the number of foreign market entry options increases. An increasing number of Chinese companies have turned to a combination of multiple modes instead of merely engaging in product exports and are operating in foreign markets through acquisition and listing, which shows how Chinese companies' growth drives internationalisation. From 2005 to 2015, 214 of 868 outward investment deals worth over US$100 million by Chinese companies were greenfield investments, and 500 were multinational acquisitions. Seven overseas M&A deals worth over US$1 billion were completed by Chinese companies in 2015, as shown in Table 9.4.

In 2000, only 26 Chinese companies went public overseas, but since China joined the WTO in 2001, a growing number of Chinese companies have entered foreign capital markets through listings abroad. With the ongoing progress of 'going global' and opening up, recent years have witnessed significant growth in the number of Chinese companies listed overseas: 115 Chinese companies went public abroad in 2010, 47 in 2011, 42 in 2012, 113 in 2013, 141 in 2014, and 142 in 2015. Most of these companies were listed on the Hong Kong Main Board, NASDAQ, NYSE, and Frankfurt Stock Exchange (FWB) (see Fig. 9.3). The industries involved have also diversified, among which finance, biotech/healthcare, and telecommunications and value-added services accounted for the highest proportions in 2015, at 21.3, 11.2, and 5.6%, respectively.

Table 9.4 Major overseas M&A deals (worth over US$1 billion) by Chinese companies in 2015

Buyer	Seller	Country	Amount	The proportion of shares purchased (%)
ChemChina	Pirelli	Italy	US$7.7 billion	26.2
Chinese consortium	Lumileds, Royal Philips	The Netherlands	US$3.3 billion	80
Bohai Leasing	Avolon (aircraft leasing)	Ireland	US$2.555 billion	100
Bright Food	Tnuva (food processing)	Israel	US$2.167 billion	77.7
Fosun International	Ironshore (insurance)	United States	US$1.84 billion	80
Wanda Group	Infront Sports and Media	Switzerland	US$1.191 billion	100
Fosun Group	Club Med	France	US$1.191 billion	98

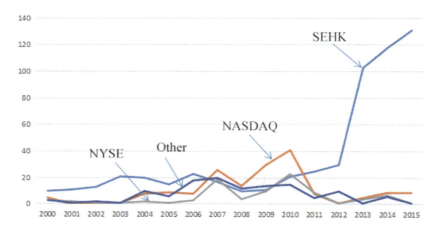

Fig. 9.3 Choice of stock exchanges for Chinese IPOs overseas, 2000–2015[1]

[1] 'Other' includes the FWB, Singapore Exchange (SGX), American Stock Exchange (AMEX), and London Alternative Investment Market (AIM).

Chinese MNEs go public overseas mainly through a direct overseas listing, placement, listing by introduction, and transfer of listing. Overseas direct listing means that a corporation directly applies for listing on a local exchange as a domestic entity. Placement is where a listed company sells a proportion of new shares to institutional investors through a private offering. Listing by introduction is an application for listing securities already in issue, where no new shares are issued and no shares held by existing shareholders are sold. Finally, transfer of listing means the transfer of a company's listing from one board to another. Other forms of overseas listing include secondary listing, back door listing, American depositary shares, placement, and public offering (see Fig. 9.4).

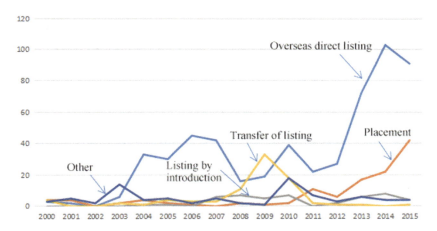

Fig. 9.4 Ways of listing overseas for Chinese companies, 2005–2015

9.2.4 Change of Parent-Subsidiary Governance Mode

An oscillation between centralisation and decentralisation has characterised the development of the parent-subsidiary relationship of Chinese MNEs. In the early stages of multinational operations dominated by exporting, the group maintained total control of the multinational business. Gradually, as resource commitments increased and entry modes diversified, MNEs began to establish branches and subsidiaries abroad. A parent company generally has more control over branches than subsidiaries, with the latter enjoying more autonomy and independence in response to institutional, legal, and cultural differences during business localisation and legitimacy acquisition. One of China's most successful MNEs, Huawei, set up the Australia Board of Directors in its local arm in 2012 to facilitate localisation and internationalisation, which is the first-ever overseas board of Huawei. The board consists of Australian business and political experts. Three independent directors were former Australian officials: Alexander Downer, former Minister for Foreign Affairs; John Brumby, former Premier of Victoria; and John Lord, retired Rear Admiral of the Australian Navy, who served as the Chairman of the Board. With the development of economic globalisation, comprehensive strategies are required to coordinate value creation activities worldwide and deal with international competition, which entails a return to centralised governance for MNEs' multinational business operations. The relationship between the parent company and its subsidiaries then becomes a priority. Accordingly, over the past ten years, the proportion of foreign directors and CEOs in Chinese overseas-listed companies rose and then declined.

9.2.5 *Development of Governance Structures*

As Chinese MNEs expand their multinational business with diverse methods of operation, multinational governance issues have come into the spotlight, with internal governance structure improvements demanded. The large number of problems arising from multinational operations have led researchers to reflect on defects in Chinese MNEs' governance structures.

Multinational governance structures evolve in terms of compliance and internationalisation. First, a sound corporate governance structure facilitates operations in the host market. China's capital market mechanisms, such as information disclosure and the protection of small and medium-sized shareholders, lag behind those of developed countries. Chinese MNEs should develop a legally compliant governance structure to acquire local legitimacy. From this perspective, Chinese MNEs' multinational operations in a sound institutional environment help improve compliance levels. For example, developed countries generally impose stricter requirements on the independent director system, financial accounting system, and information disclosure mechanism. Entry into such countries can be demanding for Chinese MNEs, but it pushes them to improve their governance structure.

There is often inadequate compliance in Chinese MNEs' governance mechanisms because they tend to be highly government-related and relationship-based. Independent directors might not be truly independent or granted enough power under a deficient organisational structure, which highlights the importance of a sound corporate governance structure as a foundation for multinational business activities. Chinese companies have been damaged by compliance problems, such as through the anti-dumping action against Sichuan Changhong Electric and the China Aviation Oil (CAO) incident.

In addition to compliance enhancement, Chinese MNEs have also made efforts at internationalisation, as manifested by a growing number of executives with international backgrounds who can use their international knowledge and resources to help companies better identify risks and opportunities and improve their multinational governance capabilities. Many Chinese MNEs recruit professionals with international educational backgrounds or working experience and even appoint foreign experts as directors or executives, and some provide incumbent executives with opportunities to study abroad. For example, Wang Shi, the founder and chairman of Vanke, chose to study overseas in 2011. An increasing number of companies have employed directors and executives with international backgrounds to facilitate international expansion. However, the pattern differs between Chinese SOEs and private companies. From 2008 to 2015, the number of overseas executives, directors, and independent directors in Chinese listed companies rose, as shown in Figs. 9.5 and 9.6.

Geely Holding Group, one of China's largest MNEs and private companies, has been operating multinationally since 2009. In 2002, the group began to introduce directors with international experience to empower its multinational operations with the required knowledge and experience. In 2009, five of its 12 board directors had international experience; in 2012, it was eight of 15; and in 2016, it was six of 12, representing a high proportion of international professionals. International experience is also a requirement for its executives in corporate management. SOEs, except for their listed or overseas subsidiaries, do not emphasise international experience as much as private companies; however, even among SOEs, international experience is becoming increasingly popular.

The evolution of the multinational governance structure of Lenovo, one of China's largest MNEs, is a good example of this tendency. The group grew into an MNE after it acquired an IBM division in 2004 and needed to adjust its corporate governance structure, business, and culture.

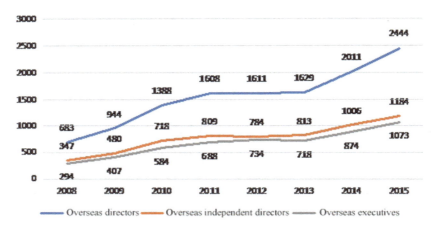

Fig. 9.5 Overseas directors, independent directors, and executives in Chinese listed companies, 2008–2015

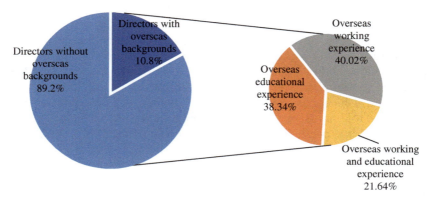

Fig. 9.6 Proportion and types of directors with overseas backgrounds in Chinese listed companies, 2015

Initially, there were changes in senior management: Yang Yuanqing, former CEO of Lenovo Group, was appointed chairman of the board, and Stephen M. Ward, former vice president of IBM's PC business, became the new CEO. The ratio of original Lenovo management to IBM's PC business staff in the new group was 7:6. After restructuring, Lenovo needed to make strategic adjustments to establish global supply chains, reduce total operating costs, and improve multinational governance capabilities to improve competitiveness. Bill Amelio, former President of Dell's Asia/Pacific Division, was appointed the new CEO, and Yang Yuanqing continued to serve as chair. Shortly afterwards, Amelio sets up a private executive team composed of foreign professionals, enabling the group to substantially improve its governance capabilities and overcome multinational acquisition and global strategic planning challenges.

Many scholars have found that executives with more international experience can promote the internationalisation of MNEs. According to Sanders and Carpenter (1998), international operations significantly impact corporate governance, as its complexity and uncertainties are accommodated by its governance structure, which suggests that firms manage and cope with the information-processing demand and agency issues arising from internationalisation. In addition, a sound corporate governance structure (mainly including the board of directors and executives) fosters MNEs' capabilities for multinational operations and helps them to gain legitimacy (Barroso et al., 2011; Rivas et al., 2009; Sherman et al., 1998).

The evolution of Chinese MNEs' multinational governance reveals that these companies attach more importance to their multinational governance as their engagement in multinational operation deepens. Furthermore, as a major part of MNEs' strategic activities, multinational operations have drawn increasing attention from management. Multinational governance is precisely the institutional arrangement aimed at overcoming internal and external challenges, success at which determines the outcome of multinational operations.

The characteristics of Chinese companies change as their multinational business expands. Despite rapid economic growth, there is still a gap between the governance performance of Chinese MNEs and that of MNEs in developed countries, which is compounded by the complexity and uncertainty of international markets. Therefore, acute pressure remains on Chinese MNEs to give more weight to institutional and cultural differences between the home and host countries. Furthermore, many Chinese MNEs, especially SOEs, rely on external governance models that are government-controlled and relationship-based. Their top priority is to shift from administrative-led to market-oriented governance, and their second priority is to design reasonable ownership and control structures. Compared with foreign MNEs, Chinese companies began multinational business later but grew faster, resulting in a mismatch between their governance capabilities and business scale. Therefore, it is crucial to enhance multinational governance capabilities, such as the management of parent-subsidiary relationships, high-level mechanism design, stakeholder governance in host countries, and the acquisition of local legitimacy.

REFERENCES

Barroso, C., Villegas, M. M., & Perez-Calero, L. (2011). Board influence on a firm's internationalisation. *Corporate Governance: An International Review, 19*(4), 351–367.

Buckley, P. J., & Casson, M. (1976). *The future of the multinational enterprise.* Holmes and Meier.

Dunning, J. H. (1977). Trade, location of economic activity and the MNE: A search for an eclectic approach. In *The international allocation of economic activity.* Palgrave Macmillan.

Huang, S. J., & Liu, J. L. (2009). Study on foreign market entry mode selection of Chinese enterprises. *China Industrial Economics, 2009*(1), 108–117.

Hymer, S. H. (1960). *The international operation of national firms: A study of direct foreign investment.* Doctoral dissertation, Massachusetts Institute of Technology.

Rivas, J. L., Hamori, M., & Mayo, M. (2009). Board composition and firm internationalisation. In *Academy of Management Annual Meeting Proceedings 2009* (pp. 1–6).

Sanders, W. M. G., & Carpenter, M. A. (1998). Internationalization and firm governance: The role of CEO compensation, top team composition, and board structure. *Academy of Management Journal, 2*(4), 158–179.

Sherman, H. D., Kashlak, R. J., & Joshi, M. P. (1998). The effect of the board and executive committee characteristics on the degree of internationalisation. *Journal of International Management, 4,* 311–335.

Tian, Z. L., Deng, X. M., & Fan, S. (2007). A research on internationalisation process of Chinese firms based on the top 500. *China Soft Science, 9,* 88–96.

Vernon, R. (1966). International investment and international trade in the product cycle. *The Quarterly Journal of Economics, 80*(2), 190–207.

Xiong, H. B., & Deng, X. M. (2010). Research on driving forces of Chinese companies' international expansion. *Business Management Journal, 32*(7), 63–69.

Zhang, S. M., & Xu, L. (2008). The empirical research on overseas entry mode and investment performance of chinese enterprises [J]. *Journal of Shandong University (Philosophy and Social Sciences),* (06), 130–136.

CHAPTER 10

Conclusions

Due to the economic globalisation, MNEs have become a major driver of international competition. Many have significantly promoted international trade and economic and technological cooperation. However, many problems have emerged in this process, such as boycotts by local consumers, sanctions imposed by local governments, class actions by foreign shareholders, strikes of local subsidiaries, and legal non-compliance, which have drawn significant public attention. In recent years, amounting anti-globalising trend of protectionism and unilateralism have hindered the expansion of MNEs, which necessitates a better understanding and further development of multinational corporate governance theories.

This book has tried to address this pressing need among the academic and business communities. First, the book provided a review of traditional MNE governance and corporate governance theories and a deeper look into the characteristics and connotations of multinational corporate governance. Second, a new conceptual framework for MNE network governance was proposed based on different MNE stakeholders' governance characteristics and modes from the perspectives of network nodes, network relationships, and external network governance. Finally, this theoretical framework was applied to analyse the structures, mechanisms, and governance paths for Chinese MNEs and forecast the future trends of multinational governance. The book has comprehensively reviewed the theories of multinational corporate governance and identified their deficiencies. It has provided theoretical guidance for further developing MNE governance theories and improving governance effectiveness in the new era based on in-depth studies of MNEs' network governance framework.

10.1 Multinational Corporate Governance Theories: Predecessors and Developments

This book has provided a systematic overview of the theoretical studies related to multinational corporate governance. The earliest theories included Hymer's (1960) monopolistic advantage theory, Buckley and Casson's (1976) internalisation theory, and Dunning's (1988) eclectic theory of international production. With the development of the global economy and the emergence of new markets, some scholars began to recognise the importance of investment experience and technological achievements of companies from emerging markets in their business activities, leading to the small-scale technology theory (Wells, 1977) and technological innovation and industrial upgrading theory (Cantwell, 1994).

Traditional MNE theories are based on studies of international trade and industrial organisations. However, an increasing number of scholars are studying how MNEs remain competitive based on theories related to corporate management, organisation, and strategies (such as organisational learning theory and real options theory). As a vital part of corporate management, corporate governance has become a core issue in MNE governance studies.

However, multinational governance displays unique features and additional complexity due to expanding organisational and institutional boundaries compared with general corporate governance. In addition, the institutional distance between the home and host countries, reflecting institutional, cultural, and economic differences, exacerbates the difficulties for MNEs in adapting to foreign markets and handling external uncertainty. Meanwhile, the diversification of governing parties resulting from extended agency chains and expanded organisational boundaries inside groups give rise to governance and compliance risks outside of home countries, along with higher complexity and coordination costs. Traditional corporate governance theories are therefore not applicable to multinational governance.

This book has reviewed and developed theories incorporating stakeholders, agency, institutional design, decision-making, and networks while drawing on existing studies to lay a theoretical foundation for further research. In addition, it has analysed the similarities and differences between multinational corporate governance, international business, and corporate governance theories based on the specific characteristics of MNE governance.

10.2 Network-Based Analytical Framework for Multinational Corporate Governance Studies

Multinational corporate governance is essentially based on a network within which the home and host countries and MNEs achieve overall coordination through a set of mechanisms and governance structures. Various governing parties (nodes) form a complex network (planes) based on their dynamic interactions (lines). For example, a parent company and a group of cross-border and geographically dispersed subsidiaries constitute the internal network of an MNE, which promotes information transmission and resource-sharing between the parent and its subsidiaries and between the subsidiaries. Foreign subsidiaries connect with local organisations in the host country to establish an external network, such as through joint ventures and strategic alliances. External networks can reduce information asymmetry and external risks for foreign subsidiaries and help them improve their adaptability (Fig. 10.1).

MNEs' network governance refers to a process of organisational optimisation and institutional design carried out by key nodes in MNE networks to reach their common goals. It includes network nodes, relationship networks, and external network governance. Network node governance is aimed at maximising corporate benefits through behaviour management and incentive and restraint mechanisms. Parent-subsidiary governance is analysed in three dimensions: the board of directors, equity, and management. Relationship network governance focuses on the relationship between a parent company and its foreign subsidiaries to dynamically balance and coordinate mutual benefits. It includes parent company strategies and parent-subsidiary governance as well as parent company control and equity governance in subsidiaries. External network governance is designed to achieve overall coordination through reasonable and standardised network operations conducted by external governing parties. It mainly concerns how the institutional environments of home and host

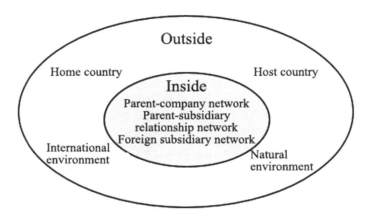

Fig. 10.1 MNE networks

countries and the institutional and cultural distance between them affect multinational corporate governance.

The network governance framework proposed in this book enriches MNE governance theories. Moreover, it captures a characteristic of MNEs' network governance highlighted in this book: the involvement of many interconnected links or sub-systems in a network, such as structures, goals, mechanisms, and effects.

10.3 Two Key Issues in Multinational Corporate Governance

Multinational corporate governance targets problems arising from the parent-subsidiary relationship and the differences between internal and external environments. The former is related to internal structural changes due to cross-border operations, whereas the latter focuses on external environmental changes.

Different strategic roles played by foreign subsidiaries lead to various types of parent-subsidiary relationships, which may give rise to various governance problems. The governance of parent-subsidiary relationships is at the core of multinational corporate governance and determines MNEs' performance and governance effectiveness; it, therefore, calls for appropriate governance structures. The institutional environment in the host country is the first challenge for MNEs in their outward investment. Local cultures, economies, and markets may affect MNEs' choices of the host country, entry mode (greenfield vs. acquisition), and legitimacy acquisition. Institutional differences between the home and host countries, also known as institutional distance, can be divided into the formal institutional differences associated with mandatory and statutory laws and regulations and the informal institutional differences associated with social norms and values (i.e., cultural distance).

The direction of institutional distance is expressed as the institutional gap. If the institutional quality in the home country is higher than that of the host country, there is an institutional surplus; if the reverse is true, there is an institutional deficit. The direction of the gap has a crucial impact on the governance of MNEs from emerging markets. Based on its concept and characteristics, this book has delved into how the institutional gap (surplus vs. deficit) affects the location of MNEs' foreign direct investment, equity entry modes, governance of equity ownership of foreign subsidiaries, and the performance of Chinese overseas listed companies, thus serving as a supplement to research on the institutional gap in multinational corporate governance.

10.4 Experience of and Aspirations for China's Multinational Corporate Governance Practices

Research into China's multinational corporate governance has advanced with the development of Chinese MNEs. In the early stages of internationalisation, most attention was paid to the role of multinational investment and operations in improving MNEs' competitiveness and international influence. Later, as the understanding of MNE governance deepened, the focus shifted to the location of multinational investment, equity governance, legitimacy acquisition, and other relevant issues. This book has summarised the structures and the internal and external mechanisms and paths of governance of Chinese MNEs and put forward the characteristics, deficiencies, and future trends of China's multinational corporate governance.

Although China's multinational corporate governance started late, there has been a rapid development in this field over recent years. For example, compliance is becoming an important factor in multinational governance structures, as evidenced by the prevalence of independent director systems, financial accounting systems, and information disclosure mechanisms. A sound governance structure is conducive to effective corporate management in the host country. Furthermore, the governance structure of Chinese MNEs has also become more international. For example, Geely started recruiting directors with international experience in 2002, and its proportion of international board members reached 50% by 2016. The group's executive team is also international.

Nonetheless, many problems have arisen in the development of Chinese MNEs' governance, such as the uneasy coexistence of administrative-led and market-oriented governance modes in SOEs, weak adaptability to foreign markets, lack of organisational legitimacy, and inadequate internal control, as well as the insufficient international experience and limited governance capabilities resulting from being late movers. How to enhance Chinese MNEs' international competitiveness and resolve the problem of poor governance capabilities at a time of rapid internationalisation has become a top priority. In recent years, Brexit, the rise of unilateralism and protectionism since 2018 and compounded by the COVID-19 pandemic have posed new challenges for research into China's multinational corporate governance. In a changing world, how should MNEs adjust their international strategies? What impact will international investments have on corporate behaviour, performance, and innovation? Which types of companies are likely to suffer the most? What should these companies do to cope with external crises and uncertainties? How will MNEs' governance structure and modes change? All of these issues are worthy of further study.

It is hoped that this book can promote theoretical studies of MNE governance and capacity building. Readers are invited to contribute to the development of multinational corporate governance theories in the new era.

REFERENCES

Buckley, P. J., & Casson, M. (1976). *The future of the multinational enterprise*. Holmes and Meier.

Cantwell, J. (1994). *Foreign direct investment in developing countries: The case of Latin America*. The Methodological Problems Raised by the Collection of FDI Data//En IRELA. 9–27.

Dunning, J. H. (1988). The eclectic paradigm of international production: A restatement and some possible extensions. *Journal of International Business Studies, 19*(1), 1–31.

Hymer, S. H. (1960). *The international operation of national firms: A study of direct foreign investment*. Doctoral dissertation, Massachusetts Institute of Technology.

Wells, L. T. (1977). *The internationalization of firms from developing countries*. MIT press.